Elizabeth Amoaa is the founder of Speciallady Awareness.

She authored her first book *The Unspoken Identity*.

Elizabeth holds a Bachelor of Laws (LLB) degree and a Master of Laws (LLM).

Furthermore, she has been honoured with an honorary doctorate for her outstanding humanitarian efforts, recognising her immense contributions to society.

Elizabeth has received several awards and recognitions in various countries, including the United Kingdom, Ghana, Kenya and many more.

Her remarkable journey as the first black woman to courageously share her personal story on a global platform has gained her a global recognition.

Born with uterus didelphys and other reproductive health disorders, she has become an inspiring advocate for raising awareness and promoting understanding of such conditions.

To every young person who feels there is no safe environment to freely speak up or seek support, I want to encourage you. Do not let your past experiences or trauma hold you back from reaching for greater heights.

Elizabeth Amoaa

THE SPECIAL LADY

AUSTIN MACAULEY PUBLISHERS™

LONDON • CAMBRIDGE • NEW YORK • SHARJAH

A CIP catalogue record for this title is available from the British Library.

ISBN 9781035843961 (Paperback)
ISBN 9781035843978 (ePub e-book)

www.austinmacauley.com

First Published 2024
Austin Macauley Publishers Ltd®
1 Canada Square
Canary Wharf
London
E14 5AA

Table of Contents

Introduction

This book that you are about to read will take you on a journey of self-transformation and teach you how to embrace obstacles as a means of overcoming life's challenges.

As we evolve in life, self-growth or self-improvement is crucial as it gives us a continuous process of learning, development and refinement that enables us to become our best selves. Self-growth involves identifying and acknowledging one's strengths and weaknesses, setting goals and taking action to achieve those goals. Self-growth can encompass a wide range of areas, including physical health, emotional well-being, intellectual development, spiritual growth and interpersonal relationships. It can be a challenging journey, but also an opportunity to learn and improve ourselves which can lead to a more fulfilling and satisfying life.

Life is full of challenges and self-growth because it can help us develop the resilience we need to overcome obstacles and bounce back from setbacks. By cultivating a growth mindset, we can learn to view challenges as opportunities for growth and development.

Self-growth can also have a positive impact on our physical health. By taking care of ourselves and making healthy lifestyle choices, we can improve our overall well-being and reduce our risk of developing health problems.

We can achieve a greater sense of purpose and meaning in life when we embark on a path of self-growth.

Chapter 1
Revelation

I possess great qualities that motivate me to strive for greatness. Overcoming childhood trauma, disappointments, failures and my health journey have moulded me into a warrior. However, I was still hindered from becoming the great woman I aspire to be.

It seems that I may have been holding back from achieving greatness, either out of fear or comfort with being known as the 'Special lady' who inspires others with my story. However, I believe that there is much more I can offer to the world and the universe rewards those who give generously. To this end, I have been learning and growing, making positive changes in my life, cutting out toxic relationships and surrounding myself with inspiring individuals who have made a difference in their communities. Despite being proud of the woman I have become after overcoming health challenges and life obstacles, I still wonder if quitting law school and prioritising my roles as a mother, wife and advocate for women with gynaecological conditions was the right decision.

There were many questions and doubts when I decided not to pursue my legal career to become an international lawyer but rather to become a reproductive health advocate.

I considered that becoming a reproductive health advocate would allow me to pursue a career or lifestyle that aligns more with my personal interests and values. My own health journey, which involved multiple surgeries, a late diagnosis and medical complications, gave me a passion for health and wellness. Pursuing a legal career did not seem to offer the same sense of fulfilment as becoming a health advocate, even though I knew that as a reproductive health advocate, I might not receive payment and my financial circumstances could be at risk. Despite this, I focused on the joy that I brought to other women who were going through similar life experiences as me and I had faith that I would somehow have a financial breakthrough to continue to do greater humanitarian work.

Moreover, the field of health advocacy is rapidly growing and offers numerous opportunities for those who are passionate about helping others live healthier lives. As a health advocate, I believed that I would one day be able to find paid work within the field while still being able to do charity work. I also dreamt of starting my own health advocacy business or consultancy.

As a reproductive health advocate, I have found that I can make a meaningful difference in people's lives by promoting healthy behaviours and lifestyles. This allows me to help individuals prevent or manage reproductive health disorders and other related health conditions. I find my work as a special lady to be highly gratifying, as it gives me a sense of purpose, fulfilment and greater satisfaction.

Life is full of tragedies, unplanned choices, and adventures. Ultimately, life is a precious gift filled with opportunities, challenges and experiences that shape who we are and the world around us. It is a journey that can be unpredictable and often requires resilience, courage and a sense of purpose to navigate. Through every journey, life is what we make of it and we have the power to create meaningful and fulfilling lives by pursuing our passions, connecting with others and embracing the beauty of the world.

At this moment, as I imagine my life, I question whether it truly aligns with the definition that I am familiar with.

On a rainy Monday evening around 10 pm, I decided to investigate the symptoms I had been experiencing despite trying various remedies such as painkillers, ointments and hot water bottles. However, my pain continued to worsen and was accompanied by a fever. I requested that my husband accompany me to the hospital, which was approximately twenty minutes away from the military barracks we lived in. During the drive, I expressed my desire for a pain-free life without any future health complications. I reflected on my previous hospitalisations, consultations and treatments that had not been successful in curing any of my health issues. As a Christian, I believed that one day God would heal me, even though I sometimes questioned if he would ever forsake me.

Starting from February 2023, I have been regularly praying and strengthening my relationship with God. As a result, my spiritual life has become more profound, and I feel grateful to have comfort in God, especially considering the numerous miraculous things He has done for me in the past. I firmly believe that the closer I am to God, the more fulfilled my life will be in the future. My husband reassured me not to be anxious about my health and life obstacles, reminding me that I am blessed to be alive despite my challenging health history. However, despite my efforts to remain calm, I couldn't help feeling concerned about the symptoms I was experiencing.

While I waited for the doctor, I pondered my aspirations and goals. My vision was to make a positive difference in the lives of women and children worldwide. Specifically, I hoped that healthcare practitioners would utilise my book as a resource to offer timely medical assistance and aid to women and girls experiencing gynaecological ailments.

After my first book was published, I had hoped that it would have a significant impact on countless people's lives, which seemed to be coming true as libraries worldwide began stocking it and it was being sold by numerous online retailers globally. Despite this initial success, the past two years of my journey have been characterised by a mixture of challenges, obstacles and achievements.

Witnessing this incredible opportunity gave me a great feeling. Many people were curious about the sales I had acquired and some even asked to borrow money from me. Both strangers and acquaintances assumed that I had experienced a breakthrough and become a millionaire.

As I watched people entering and leaving doctors consultation rooms from the hospital reception area, I continued to experience excruciating pain. Despite this, my thoughts turned to my life over the past two years, which had felt like an entire lifetime. Even though I had become an author by sharing my abnormality (uterus didelphys), living with endometriosis stage four, secondary infertility and other reproductive health disorders, I had expected my life's uncertainties to come to an end. However, life kept reminding me that it is a journey of learning, with trials, setbacks and tribulations, as well as joy, breakthroughs and success.

Chapter 2
Life Changing

In 2021, I joined Rotary International with the aim of collaborating with like-minded individuals who are dedicated to promoting humanitarian efforts and creating sustainable change across the globe. Although initially hesitant when my friend Dr Patrick suggested I join, I was mainly concerned about whether I would acquire the necessary knowledge and skills to aid me in my personal development and passion for promoting adequate healthcare among women and young girls.

My experience with the Rotary has been transformative as I have had the privilege of connecting with extraordinary people who have supported my advocacy work and assisted me in promoting *The Unspoken Identity* book.

I have successfully been involved in community projects with other like-minded organisations and individuals from various Rotary clubs.

Through Rotary, I met Tim and his wife Janice, who have been a tremendous source of encouragement and have helped me unlock my full potential. It was an honour to have my story and debut book *The Unspoken Identity* featured in the Rotary International Great Britain and Ireland magazine.

Being a Rotarian enabled me to meet new and existing members to enhance my knowledge, skills and capacity to contribute effectively to my club and community.

Furthermore, Rotary provides me a platform to showcase my projects, achievements and impact to a wider audience. This opportunity enhance the visibility of my non-governmental organisations Speciallady Awareness's activities, both in Ghana and beyond leading to an increase in awareness, support and engagement with various agencies and other non-governmental organisations.

My first book *The Unspoken Identity* featured in Rotary International Great Britain and Ireland magazine reached out to over 40,000 members in over 1,500 clubs, which was a marvellous opportunity to share my story and book to encourage other women to seek early diagnosis and appropriate treatment for their gynaecological conditions.

Rotarians volunteer their time and talents to tackle challenges globally by promoting peace, fighting disease and working towards sustainable growth and change in the world.

From the year 2020, various award bodies recognised my philanthropic and advocacy work.

I managed to receive ten awards and recognitions as well as my charity for promoting reproductive health rights among women and young girls and combating menstrual poverty.

Before the year 2020, I had made plans with my NGO Speciallady Awareness team to travel to Ghana and conduct outreach projects in Wiamoase, Accra and Akwamu Adumasa during Easter in April 2020.

We planned to carry out a community outreach programme in Amasaman to donate toys, books and drinks to thousands of children.

Moreover, radio interviews and TV shows were arranged for me to appear on to promote the advocacy work and outreach projects we intended to do during the Easter holidays in Ghana. It was an exciting opportunity and I was thrilled to collaborate with individuals who were passionate about helping others.

Our mission was to distribute sanitary products to women and girls to address menstrual poverty, as well as raise awareness about gynaecological disorders and promote reproductive health rights. I was excited about the trip, especially since it coincided with the Wiamoase Homecoming 2020.

However, the world was hit with a tragedy, the Covid-19 pandemic outbreak.

The Covid-19 pandemic was a global health crisis that has affected virtually every aspect of daily life. The Covid-19 pandemic had a significant impact on public health, the global economy and social norms.

Many countries had to implement strict measures to curb the spread of the virus, such as lockdowns, travel restrictions and social distancing guidelines.

The Covid-19 pandemic had a significant global health crisis that affected virtually every aspect of daily life. This catastrophic event prevented me from travelling to Ghana. All the outreach activities planned for Wiamoase Homecoming were cancelled due to the lockdown and cancellation of flights.

I made a choice to engage in humanitarian efforts in order to provide aid to women and children who were impacted by the Covid-19 pandemic. Although I could not travel, I managed to get volunteers in Ghana to help with the donations.

Through my organisation, Speciallady Awareness, we partnered with a renowned media personality in Ghana called Abeiku Santana to provide food for thousands of vulnerable individuals in Accra and the surrounding areas. We utilised social media platforms to both raise awareness of the pandemic and collect funds for our cause. Numerous other humanitarian initiatives were undertaken by various international organisations, individuals and government officials, which demonstrated a heartening sense of mutual support and compassion. Overall, it was uplifting to witness such a strong spirit of solidarity and empathy among people.

Although I couldn't be there in person for the donations, it did not feel quite the same. However, I recognised that the travel restrictions were necessary to control the spread of the virus and as someone who advocates for reproductive health, it was important for me to lead by example and follow the rules. In 2020, my NGO Speciallady Awareness donated sanitary products, toiletries and medical supplies worth thousands of pounds to the 37 Military Hospital in Ghana to support the delivery of essential medical care for women and paediatric patients. We received support from the advocate for the World Health Organisation, which provided us with medical supplies.

Despite facing challenging financial difficulties due to the loss of most of our sponsors and donors amidst the global economic crisis caused by the Covid-19 pandemic, Speciallady Awareness was able to continue its outreach projects. We used various fundraising techniques to raise funds and successfully completed almost every project we decided to partake in.

Overcoming

While experiencing the effects of the Covid-19 pandemic outbreak, I found myself becoming increasingly anxious about my health. Even though my health concerns did not place me in the vulnerable group for Covid-19, I remained worried about my well-being. This is because I have a weakened immune system due to a low red blood cell count, which makes me more susceptible to infections and I often suffer from fatigue, dizziness and chronic pains. I suspect that my low red blood cell count may have been as a result of my rare congenital abnormality called uterus didelphys, which means I have two wombs, two cervixes and two vaginal canals.

I suffer from a severe form of endometriosis known as rectovaginal endometriosis, which is less common, but more severe. This occurs when the tissue that lines the uterus grows into the tissues between the rectum and vagina, as well as into the rectum and vagina themselves. Additionally, I also have endometriosis in the area around my lower bowel and sacrum ligament.

In addition to having endometriosis, I also have around eight uterine fibroids and adhesions. Managing the symptoms of these conditions can be both unpredictable and painful. I began to notice that my symptoms were worsening, including bleeding between periods and experiencing more painful and irregular menstrual cycles. Although I was scheduled to have surgery, there were several appointment cancellations in the gynaecology unit, which was taking a toll on me emotionally and mentally. My doctor became concerned, particularly with the irregular menstrual cycles and spotting that occurred after my monthly period. To rule out any potential health issues such as cancer or kidney problems, she ordered blood and urine tests, which left me anxious about the results.

Thankfully, everything came back clear.

From the end of the year 2018 to 2020, I was engaged in a legal battle for medical malpractice in relation to a procedure I underwent in 2017. Specifically, I had a coil inserted for contraceptive and endometriosis management purposes, but the procedure resulted in significant trauma and distress. Throughout the legal process, my solicitors worked tirelessly to secure a just and satisfactory outcome for me.

The legal battle has had a significant impact on me, especially when I recall the incident and realise that it could have been prevented easily if the consultant had provided proper advice. However, the more I think about the incident, the more painful it becomes.

It was determined that the consultant admitted to failing to advise me on the dangers of IUD insertion and its complications, particularly in a woman with my type of anatomy. As a result, there was a higher chance of uterus perforation or other medical complications.

Why did the doctor halt the procedure upon realising that my anatomy was not the type he had encountered during his tenure in gynaecology? Additionally, why did he not communicate his findings to me after I regained consciousness from the anaesthesia, and instead assured me that everything went well except for the inability to insert a coil into the left uterine due to its narrowness?

Despite my efforts to obtain answers from solicitors and medical professionals involved in my case, I did not receive the information I was seeking. Instead, all I heard were apologies. Although I received some form of compensation, it was not enough to compensate for the pain, trauma, and distress caused by the consultant.

Despite the challenges I've faced, I became more grateful to be alive and able to make a positive impact on the lives of others. As I murmured these words to myself, I couldn't help but reflect on my journey. Although the consultant may have caused my health problems, I am determined to use my second chance at life to fulfil my purpose on this earth. I decided to remain strong and positive, fighting for a pain-free lifestyle and encouraging other women to seek early diagnosis and appropriate treatment to prevent them from experiencing what I've gone through.

The worst part of my case was when it was established that I had suffered a hole during the procedure of the coil insertion, which I was not informed about. All these complications could have been prevented if the consultant had carried out ultrasounds when I presented myself to him following the evacuation of my womb after a silent miscarriage in 2017. The more they read the verdict, the more upsetting it sounded. It was obvious the consultant used my rare congenital abnormality as grounds for the negligence he caused instead of taking full accountability for his actions.

It was brought to my attention that the severity of the endometriosis was going to cause other severe complications with or without the consultant's actions.

It was also noted that due to my anatomy, I was at high risk for other reproductive health disorders and I already had secondary infertility.

I was angry and disappointed with the medical professionals, but my faith kept me strong.

The more they read the verdict, the more upsetting it sounded. It was obvious that the consultant had used my rare congenital abnormality as grounds for the negligence they caused, instead of taking full accountability for their actions. However, it was brought to my attention that the severity of my endometriosis was going to cause other severe complications regardless of the consultant's actions. Additionally, it was noted that due to my anatomy, I was at high risk for other reproductive health disorders and I was already experiencing secondary infertility. Although I was angry and disappointed with the medical professionals, my faith kept me strong.

I recall one day, while lying in bed contemplating about my health conditions, disappointments and challenges I made a decision to seek help for my mental health.

In the morning, I spoke to my doctor about the possibility of getting a therapist. She listened attentively and commended me for taking the initiative to seek support and share my experiences related to my health journey. In the past, I had declined offers of therapy because I didn't want to feel like a failure, victim or patient with various health issues. However, this time, I knew it was necessary.

My doctor made the referral and also encouraged me to consider self-referral to I Talk. When I searched for them on the internet and their website popped up on my laptop screen, I felt a wave of panic and almost backed out.

I became tearful while typing the reason for my self-referral on the I Talk enquiry form. It was a brief, distressing statement in which I requested to speak to someone about my journey and trauma. Within 24 hours, I received an email and a follow-up phone call. However, the phone conversation was very unsettling as it lasted an hour and I was asked a lot of questions about why I needed help.

As I began narrating a few incidents that have had psychological effects on me, I found myself bursting into tears. I was given some time to relax and pour out my pain and the one-hour conversation felt like a lifetime. I was advised to undergo cognitive behavioural therapy (CBT), also known as talking therapy, to help me manage my problems by changing the way I think and behave. I was offered twelve sessions, which were subject to review if I needed further treatment.

On the first day of the session, the first few minutes were quite casual. However, as we delved deeper into the discussion, I began to break down more. Opening up about my journey, including my childhood, my perspective on life and my health journey, was quite upsetting.

However, I realised that it was time for me to be honest with myself and accept help. As I opened up, I began to understand that I have been experiencing anxiety and depression and I realised that seeking help was crucial in dealing with mental health issues. One of the most stressful parts was talking about the silent miscarriage I experienced in 2017 and undergoing multiple surgeries, which did not cure me but resulted in more complications.

When I started to talk about the IUD insertion that ended up causing damage to one of my wombs and complications, I cried excessively. I then realised that the experience had traumatised me. Although I did not want to accept that the consultant's actions did not define me and had not mentally broken me, it was obvious that I was suffering psychologically from the incident.

The therapist provided exceptional support, actively listening to my thoughts, feelings and experiences during our sessions. As I engaged with the assignments, I found myself opening up more, allowing me to release some painful experiences from my past. I envisioned a life as a child free from pain, with a loving family and a safe environment, without the judgement of being different. One without obstacles, setbacks, failures and disappointments.

As I envisioned a new way of life, I began to understand my true nature and how I could create positive changes by embracing my challenging experiences as opportunities for self-transformation. Instead of feeling sorry for myself or questioning my identity, I realised that I could become the best version of myself. Through CBT sessions, I learnt that I cannot undo the past, but I can focus on the future and strive for better days ahead.

Reflecting on my charity work, personal achievements and my role as a mother to my daughter, I have come to realise that some of my painful past experiences have shaped me into the woman I am today. Although it may be tempting to believe that such tragedies do not affect us, it is impossible to completely block the impact of past hurt and trauma, especially when there have not been adequate solutions or remedies to correct those issues.

As 2020 came to an end, I found myself smiling to the outside world while crying within. I knew things could be better, but I felt powerless to change them. I was struggling mentally but felt ashamed to open up to the people.

Especially since I was the voice for women and young girls suffering from gynaecological conditions, I felt it was my duty to act strong and stay positive for others to follow my example in seeking early medical intervention. However, I soon realised that keeping my true feelings to myself was affecting me. As someone from an African background, mental health issues are rarely discussed, making it easier to stay silent than to expose what was going on with me. Despite my past experiences, I thought I was strong enough to handle any life obstacle. I felt that people on social media were watching me, wanting to see only the best parts of my life and achievements and not my struggles. I retreated into a bubble where I continued to question my healing process and past traumas as a way of dealing with my inner feelings.

Despite my husband's inquiry about my well-being, I dishonestly claimed that I was handling everything fine. Also, seeing my personal story circulating on the internet was a challenging time for me, particularly when I came across negative feedback.

Although I was pleased that my story was positively influencing people, the social media attention was overwhelming and I still felt a sense of emptiness knowing that I would have to live with ongoing medical complications.

Therefore, the CBT sessions served as a means to evaluate my genuine emotions and comprehension of being an advocate for women and young girls.

However, after completing CBT sessions, I felt empowered with the tools given to me by the therapist to combat future setbacks.

The Covid-19 pandemic brought me in contact with incredible people virtually, many of whom were like-minded individuals. I was thrilled to connect with influential personalities from various communities, both in the United Kingdom and abroad.

I was honoured that many young people chose me as a mentor. Using my own life experiences to inspire and guide them towards achieving their goals and visions is a fulfilling experience. I've realised that my own misfortunes have become a motivational tool for others to become the best version of themselves. When I listen to these young people's struggles and life experiences, I am confident and eager to help them change their lives for the better.

I discovered that being a mentor is crucial for personal and professional growth, both for the mentor and the mentee. As a mentor, I knew I had the opportunity to share my knowledge, experience and skills with someone who can benefit from it. By guiding and supporting someone in their journey, I knew I could help them develop their strengths, overcome their weaknesses and achieve their goals. Additionally, being a mentor allows me to improve my communication and leadership skills and gain a fresh perspective on my own experiences.

I perceived mentoring as a way of giving back to the community. Ultimately, by being a mentor, it could make a positive impact on both the mentee and me by creating a mutually beneficial relationship that fosters growth and development.

I feel privileged for the opportunities and recognition I have received from people. Although I've faced agonising challenges, I believe they were worth it for the personal growth and learning that came from those experiences. Ultimately, growth requires continuous improvement and learning from every aspect of our life journey.

Chapter 3
New Beginnings

Encountering His Royal Majesty Odeneho Kwafo Akoto III was a great honour, as he became a mentor and father figure to me. He is the highly respected King of Akwamuman, one of the oldest Akan States in Ghana and a visionary leader who advocates for better education, targeted tourism and the development of entrepreneurship skills for the welfare of his people. His commitment to philanthropic work, including founding the Odeneho Kwafo Akoto III Foundation, has inspired me to pursue my passion for changing the lives of young people across the world.

Meeting him was a true blessing. He became my confidant and guide as I embarked on a journey of learning and growth. I was fortunate to learn from a man who was not only wise but also charismatic.

Through him, I was introduced to his community and had the honour of meeting Her Majesty Paramount Queen Mother of Akwamu Traditional Area, Nana Afrakoma II. She is one of the longest-serving Queen Mothers in Ghana, having been enstooled since 1964.

Meeting prominent individuals like Her Majesty Nana Afrakoma II and His Majesty Odeneho Kwafo Akoto III is a profound experience that offers the opportunity to gain insights and knowledge from their wisdom and experiences.

Great influential personalities often have a wealth of knowledge and experience that they have accumulated over their lifetimes. By encountering and engaging with them, I am confident that I can gain insights and lessons that can help me in my own personal and professional life.

I believe that meeting influential personalities can provide me with opportunities to expand my network and connect with like-minded individuals. Through these connections, I have discovered new opportunities for collaboration, mentorship and personal growth. Interacting with other influential individuals has been a source of inspiration and motivation for me. Their stories of perseverance and success have inspired me to pursue my own goals and dreams. Additionally, these encounters have helped me build confidence and resilience.

Moreover, joining the Rotary Club has been an incredible experience for me. Not only has it allowed me to interact with influential and successful individuals, but it has also helped to build my confidence and self-esteem. By engaging with accomplished people, I have gained a sense of validation and belief in my own abilities. These interactions have created numerous opportunities for my personal and professional growth.

Through learning from their experiences and wisdom, expanding my network, finding inspiration and motivation and building confidence, I have been able to become a better version of myself and achieve greater success in life.

In celebration of the month of love in February 2021, I made the decision to donate to the people of my hometown,

Wiamoase, located in the Ashanti Region of Ghana. I donated food, toys and essential items to over two hundred orphans in Wiamoase and its surrounding towns.

Prior to this, I had been working on feeding projects in rural areas of Accra, where I was able to provide hundreds of people with meals on a quarterly basis. These feeding projects were my way of expressing gratitude for the blessings and accomplishments in my life.

I firmly believe that giving back to the community is essential for contributing to the well-being and development of the society we live in. It acknowledges the fact that we are all interdependent and that we have a responsibility to support those who may be less fortunate than ourselves. Giving back can take many forms, such as volunteering, donating money or resources, sharing skills and expertise, or simply being kind and helpful to others.

By giving back, we can address social issues, promote positive change and build stronger, more cohesive communities. It also provides us with a sense of personal fulfilment, purpose and connection. The more we give back to our communities, the better future we create for ourselves and others.

Giving back is not only an act of kindness but also a responsibility. It helps us create a more equitable and just society where everyone can thrive.

In response to the Covid-19 pandemic, there have been restrictions on donations of medical supplies and services. This catastrophic event resulted in a shortage of medical resources in many communities, particularly in countries where healthcare practitioners struggle to access the resources needed to provide essential medical care.

In 2021, these tragic circumstances motivated my NGO, Speciallady Awareness, to donate wheelchairs, sanitisers and other essentials to the Atimpoku District Health Directorate. As part of this effort, we provided twenty wheelchairs to clinics in the community.

Speciallady Awareness was involved in lots of community outreach projects and donated severally to support underprivileged communities.

Although funding was limited, we ensured we pushed our limits to continue the work Speciallady Awareness started. It was no easy feat, but we were determined to make a difference in the lives of those who needed our support the most. We rallied our team and worked tirelessly, often going above and beyond what was expected of us. We reached out to our community and made every effort to raise awareness and gather resources for our cause. Despite the challenges we faced, we never lost sight of our goal and persevered until we achieved success. Through our hard work and dedication, we were able to make a real impact and help those in need. We proved that even with limited resources, anything is possible if you have the passion and drive to make a difference.

Unexpected Outcomes

During the same year, I was thrilled to learn that I would be signed off from hospital obstetrics and gynaecology care. One morning, I woke up feeling excited about what the day had to offer. I realised that my chronic pains had slowed down and that I rarely experienced any pain anymore. It dawned on me that the last time I had experienced pain was over four months ago. I guess I had been so busy with my work at Speciallady Awareness that I hadn't even noticed.

On that same day, I had a phone call with my specialist from the hospital, during which he asked me how I was coping with my health. He also provided me with the results of some ultrasounds and an MRI scan that I underwent a few weeks ago.

During the call, I expressed my happiness with the progress of my health. When the specialist finally told me that he did not see the need for me to undergo another surgical procedure, I was thrilled. I knew that my body could not handle a seventh procedure and I was tired of the multiple surgeries that only provided short-term relief while worsening my health complications after a few months.

Knowing that my medical file was sent back to my local doctor and that I didn't have to worry about my health was a tremendous relief for my emotional well-being. I thanked God and felt eager to share the good news with my loved ones.

Living a life full of uncertainty can be a challenging experience, but it can also be an opportunity for growth and learning. For many years, I have lived with a constant worry about what the future holds. My health, life goals and relationships have been sources of anxiety and an insightful journey.

Despite the challenges, my journey through uncertainty has taught me to embrace the unknown. It has allowed me to develop resilience and learn to adapt to change. Instead of letting my fears control me, I have learnt to take risks and to be open to new opportunities.

While living with uncertainty, I have learnt that instead of worrying about what might happen, I should rather focus on what I can control and take steps to move forward.

This has helped me find purpose in even the most challenging situations.

I am aware that my health journey has helped me to build resilience. By having the ability to bounce back from adversity. Building resilience has helped me to cope with uncertainty and navigate difficult situations.

It is normal to question your purpose and goals on this earth during challenging times. However, this can be an opportunity to reflect on your passions and find your true calling.

Not only was my health improving, but I was also receiving awards and recognition for my philanthropic and advocacy work. These acknowledgements encouraged me to keep making a positive impact on people's lives.

The awards increased my motivation, receiving the awards and recognitions boosted my motivation and drove me to continue excelling in my advocacy work.

It served as validation for my efforts and inspired me to push even harder to achieve greater goals.

The awards and recognitions helped establish my credibility and expertise in the women's reproductive health field. I realised that being recognised for my good deeds served as a testament to my skills and accomplishments and provided a competitive edge when seeking employment promotions, or other opportunities in the future.

The recognitions improved my reputation and profile, I became more known for my achievements which enhanced my reputation and helped me gain visibility.

This can lead to increased networking opportunities and open doors to new career prospects.

I noticed the more recognition I get the more it increases my self-esteem.

These awards and recognitions boosted my self-esteem and sense of self-worth. Knowing that my efforts are being acknowledged and appreciated can provide a sense of pride and fulfilment.

I was happy when His Majesty Odeneho Kwafo Akoto III invited me to visit his community to continue with the Speciallady Awareness initiatives. As soon as the Covid-19 pandemic lockdown restrictions were lifted, I made arrangements to travel to Ghana and carry out outreach projects. In September 2021, the Speciallady Awareness team visited six schools located in the Asuogyaman Atimpoku District in the Eastern Region of Ghana. We were warmly welcomed in Akwamu as we embarked on our mission to promote reproductive health rights among women and young girls.

Our mission was to educate both students on the signs and symptoms of reproductive health disorders and the importance of seeking early medical intervention and support. During our visit, we also provided the students with donations of sanitary products and medical supplies to help support their health needs.

Five thousand pupils received sanitary products to tackle the issue of menstrual health and poverty.

We ensured we educated the students and people in the community on the importance of reproductive health education.

This education is critical for individuals of all ages and genders as it provides information and resources for making informed decisions about sexual and reproductive health. The education can help promote sexual health by providing information on contraception, STIs and safe sexual practices. This can help individuals make informed decisions about their sexual health and reduce the risk of unintended pregnancies and sexually transmitted infections. Also, it empowers individuals by providing them with knowledge and skills to take control of their sexual and reproductive health. It can help individuals understand their rights and responsibilities regarding sexual and reproductive health and make informed decisions about their bodies.

The students asked many questions on understanding the purpose of reproductive health education.

Speciallady Awareness team explained how the education helps reduce stigma and discrimination surrounding sexual and reproductive health issues.

I am aware of how challenging it can be for individuals to discuss sensitive topics, such as reproductive health. That's why, when I visit schools or communities with my team, I draw on my personal experiences as a woman living with various gynaecological conditions to provide understanding and support to those who may also be facing reproductive health challenges.

Notably, reproductive health education can help individuals access the healthcare they need by providing information about available resources and services. This can help ensure that individuals receive appropriate care and support for their sexual and reproductive health needs, which is the mission of Speciallady Awareness.

I believe sharing my journey and trauma will help empower individuals, reduce stigma, improve access to healthcare and support overall well-being.

Chapter 4
The Discovery of
My Royal Roots

I woke up feeling miserable one morning, still mesmerised by the dream I had the previous night. It did not feel like an ordinary dream; it was more like a vision, or perhaps a warning or a request for conquest. I could not stop thinking about its meaning.

I turned to my husband for help in interpreting the dream, but his response only unsettled me further. So, I decided to speak to one of my aunties who is knowledgeable about our family's history.

I called my auntie and asked her to be completely honest with me about everything I needed to know. I explained that the dream was related to our family history and that I needed her help in understanding its significance. She asked me to share the details of the dream and I did so. Before proceeding, I asked her to promise me that she would be truthful in her answers.

My auntie is the person I confide in the most. She is one of my mother's elder sisters and I call her the 'Iron Lady' because she's fierce, kind-hearted and full of wisdom. She inspires me to become a woman of substance and an inspiration to others.

My Auntie Grace has lived through many experiences, gaining valuable wisdom and knowledge over time. During challenging times, she offers guidance and support, providing a perspective that comes with her age and experience.

She has always been a great resource for learning about my family's history and heritage. She tells stories and memories of relatives who are no longer with us and can share their knowledge of my family's traditions and customs. I feel blessed to have her and my other auntie in France. Both of my aunties and I share a special bond and they provide a sense of unconditional love and support that can be a source of comfort during difficult times.

Auntie Grace serves as a positive role model to me and other members of the family by demonstrating how we should live a fulfilling life.

Both my aunties always bring joy and laughter into my life. They are playful and have a youthful spirit that helps me to stay positive and optimistic sometimes.

Although I have great aunties, I often find myself hesitant to share my personal issues with them, even when they make an effort to encourage me to open up. While I appreciate their concern and support, I sometimes prefer to keep certain things private and handle them on my own. However, I recognise the importance of having a supportive network and I do confide in them when I feel comfortable doing so. It's a delicate balance between personal boundaries and trusting relationships and I am learning to navigate it as I grow and mature.

However, I knew the dream needed interpretation and Auntie Grace is skilled at interpreting even the most difficult situations and enigmatic dreams. I often say that she has a special gift and she always tells me that I am a unique individual with a calling to make a positive impact in the world. Her consistent prayers and words of encouragement have been invaluable to me in my philanthropic and advocacy work.

I narrated the dream to my auntie Grace. "I had a dream about an elderly woman who asked me to search for my history and discover who I truly was and where I came from. In the dream, I heard a loud voice telling me to wake up and explore why I am known as 'The Special Lady'." I continued telling my aunt about the dream and after a while, she murmured and said ok. She asked me what was I thinking about such a dream and why I needed to know about the dream. She tried to avoid my following questions. But I was adamant to know the meaning.

I remember after waking up from the dream, I began reflecting on its meaning. I realised that I already knew why I called myself The Special Lady. It was because I was born with a rare congenital abnormality that included having two wombs, two cervixes and two vaginal canals. I also went through a journey of uncertainty to discover this condition, as well as other reproductive health disorders and complications.

The dream made me think about how important it is to know and understand our own history and identity. It was a reminder to continue exploring my roots and embrace my uniqueness.

I came to understand that I was unique. During my visits to the hospital for consultations and medical examinations, some of the medical practitioners who performed ultrasound scans or read my notes would call me 'one of a kind'. As a result, I earned the nickname 'Special Lady', denoting my distinctiveness.

I was waiting for my Auntie Grace to say something, but she remained quiet for a while. Eventually, I decided to ask her if she understood the dream. She replied with a no, but something in me urged me to seek her guidance.

I asked her a series of questions about our origins and ancestry, wondering why I did not know much about them. Auntie Grace chuckled and said, "Elizabeth, you always love to dig deeper, don't you? While I admire your curiosity and fearless attitude, sometimes it's best not to know everything."

She went on to explain that what mattered most was that we were alive and happy in the present moment.

Her response was not what I had hoped for and I suspected that there was more to it. Remaining calm, I explained to her how important it was for me to understand fully. I shared with her my occasional doubts about my calling and my struggles to comprehend the fearlessness and determination that drive my actions. Although being The Special Lady is incredibly fulfilling, I felt that delving deeper into my roots and origins would help me stay focused and make an even greater impact on the world.

I asked her if anyone in our family has ever done what I have—come out globally and shared my story, established Speciallady Awareness and used my journey to encourage other women and young girls to seek early diagnosis and treatment. It's not a common path and I feel like there must be a deeper reason driving me to make an impact in this way. I feel like there's something within me that I need to understand before I can fully embrace my strength, even in the face of challenging circumstances.

She spoke softly and said, "My daughter, I understand you perfectly and you are right."

Then, she asked if I knew who my grandmother was, to which I quickly replied, "Of course." The woman resembled my mother so much that she could have been a replica of her. She then inquired about my grandmother's mother, to which I replied that I had heard her name was Gyabuaa and that she had given birth to around ten children, one of whom happened to be my grandmother.

I also heard that she was gifted in herbal remedies and used them to help women who were infertile or had reproductive health issues. When I asked my auntie about my ancestry, she told me that she was proud of me and knew that one day I would want to understand who I really was. I then asked about Gyabuaa's mother, as I had never heard of her before. It seemed that after Gyabuaa, the family did not really talk about the ancestry tree. My auntie warned me not to start digging too deep because she knew that my curiosity would make me want to know more.

I told her that I would not, but I just wanted to understand the history.

She continued, "Well, Gyabuaa was a princess and her mother's family, which is also my maternal family, possesses the 'Sanehene' stool in Agona Ashanti."

She confirmed that Gyabuaa's father was the brave Paramount Chief Nana Akwasi Acheampong of Ashanti Agona in the Ashanti Region of Ghana.

When I asked her why we never visited the palace and why our family never talked about this part of our history, her answers became brief. She explained that Gyabuaa left the palace and settled in Wiamoase, her mother's hometown, so the family didn't know the reason behind her decision. Moreover, she did not expect me to research it, but she has shared my roots with me.

It was quite a shock to learn about my family history. Some parts did not make sense, while others helped me understand my bravery and fierce attitude. I thanked my auntie for sharing the information with me, but I also expressed my desire to learn more.

However, she started lecturing me, warning me not to search for that part of the family since they had never come looking for us. I respectfully disagreed, explaining that I believe it's important to know your roots.

The following day, I started researching the meaning of Asona my clan, 'Sanaahene', the Ashanti Agona Stool, etc.

I have always known I am Ashanti Asona clan. The symbol of the Asona is the crow or wild boar. Asona is one of the eight main Akan clans. It is said that people belonging to this clan are gifted with high levels of intelligence.

The symbolic quality of the Asona clan is statesmanship and patriotism, which is displayed by Asona Ashanti women.

The Asona clan is one of the few families in Ghana that has a tradition of allowing women to assume leadership roles as kings or chiefs. A notable example of this was Nana Yaa Asantevwaa, who ruled over Edweso (Ejisu) from 1896 to 1900. In 1900; she led the Ashanti War, also known as the War of the Golden Stool, against the British Empire.

In addition, I understood that 'Sanaahene' is the title given to the royal treasurer. The title is used primarily in Ghana and is given to a traditional ruler who is considered capable of leading the warring groups of the area. The Sanaahene is mandated to aid the Paramount Chief of an area in the performance of his duty.

After gaining some initial understanding through research, I became interested in learning more about the Agona traditional area. I conducted extensive online research.

According to history, Okomfo Anokye was enstooled as the chief of Agona because Asantehene Osei Tutu I asked the kingmakers of Agona to consider and enstool his friend Okomfo Anokye as they did not have an immediate heir to the Agona stool but rather had assigned a regent.

This same stool happened to be the one my great-grandfather was an heir and enstooled.

During my findings, it was noted that my great-great-grandfather Nana Akwasi Acheampong II was enstooled three times as the Paramount Chief of Agona.

I asked myself why he was enstooled three times. I suspected there was a good reason why Nana Akwasi Acheampong II was enstooled three times. One possible reason is that he might have voluntarily stepped down from his position as the Paramount Chief for personal reasons. Another reason could be that he might have been deposed or removed from his position as chief due to disagreements with other members of the community, or as a result of conflicts or power struggles within the community.

I murmured to myself that there was a possibility that Nana Akwasi Acheampong II was re-enstooled as a result of popular demand or support from the community, who saw him as the rightful leader of the tribe.

But I know that without conclusive or more information about the specific circumstances surrounding his enstoolment and stepping down, it is difficult to say exactly why he was enstooled three times. I began to inquire from prominent people I knew, but they were not able to provide me with the answers I needed. Then, I remembered a family friend whose uncle was an author and had written several books on the Ashanti Kingdom.

I contacted Kofi Asante who kindly gave me his uncle's contact Master Osei Kwadwo.

Master Osei Kwadwo is an author; some of his books are *A Handbook on Asante Culture, An Outline of Asante History*, and many more.

I quickly dialled the man's number and he answered with a warm greeting. After introducing myself and mentioning my hometown, he revealed that it was also his hometown. I explained the purpose of my call that afternoon and asked if he could share any information about my great-grandfather, Nana Akwasi Acheampong II.

He kindly told me that he remembered the name very well and knew quite a lot about his reign. He confirmed that Nana Akwasi Acheampong II was enstooled as the Paramount Chief in 1896, then again from 1915 to 1920, and finally from 1942 to 1958. When I asked why he was enstooled three times, he explained that during his first enstoolment, he was young and voluntarily stepped down for his elder brother to reign. He returned in 1915 when he felt he was ready to be the Paramount Chief, but something happened, and he had to step down again. However, the community could not find any suitable ruler, and they brought him back. He also mentioned that my great-great-grandfather was very brave and kind-hearted and how he was a significant figure in the history of the Agona community and his leadership was highly valued by the people.

Master Osei Kwadwo informed me that he could send me one of his books which confirmed the dates of Nana Akwasi Acheampong II's reign.

I was overjoyed to learn more about my family's history.

However, the following days were quite unsettling as I couldn't stop thinking about why the princess left the palace and why she did not return to her father's side of the family. I also wondered why her mother chose to stay in Agona and whether she returned to Wiamoase.

Despite my aunt's attempts to provide more information, I did not get any concrete details. I continued my search online, but there was very little information available about Agona Ashanti stool occupants.

Despite this, I did have some affirmations about certain aspects of my family's history.

Knowing my royal family history became an important affirmation for me.

My findings created a cultural heritage.

I realised my royal family history is a part of my cultural heritage and it can help me understand the customs, traditions and values that have been passed down through generations of my family. This knowledge can help me feel more connected to my ancestors and give me a greater sense of identity.

Also, knowing my royal family history could be a source of personal pride, especially since Nana Akwasi Acheampong II played important roles in shaping his community history. Having learnt about my great-grandmother and great-great-grandfather's accomplishments and contributions has helped me appreciate my family's place on this earth and I feel a sense of ownership over my heritage.

I can testify that my research on my royal heritage gave me an understanding of my royal family history which can help me gain a deeper appreciation for the historical context in which my ancestors lived. This will definitely influence my understanding of social, political and economic factors that shaped their lives and decisions.

Moreover, learning about my royal family history has been a source of inspiration. I discovered that my ancestors overcame incredible obstacles, made bold decisions and achieved great success despite difficult circumstances. This inspires me to overcome my own challenges and pursue my dreams with greater determination and resilience.

As a result of my research, I reached out to my friend Eva, who also comes from a royal family, for more information. I shared with Eva my decision to learn more about my heritage and the importance of understanding my identity.

In response, Eva asked me if everything was alright and why I suddenly felt the need to find answers to these questions.

I shared with her my dream and my desire to understand its interpretation. She confirmed that she sometimes wonders where my brave attitude comes from.

Eva's calm demeanour and wide range of knowledge make her an excellent friend to have around. She is someone who you can always turn to for advice, guidance, or simply a listening ear.

Despite her vast knowledge, Eva is never condescending or patronising towards others. She understands that everyone has their own unique experiences and perspectives and she is always willing to learn from them. Her humility and open-mindedness make her a truly exceptional friend.

Eva's strength of character also makes her a reliable and trustworthy friend. She is someone who always keeps her promises and follows through on her commitments. Eva's combination of intelligence, calmness, humility and reliability make her an outstanding friend. Whether you need a shoulder to cry on or someone to bounce ideas off of, she is always there for you.

After attentively listening to my story about reclaiming my royal heritage, she expressed her understanding of my reasons and offered to connect me with someone she believed could help me find information about my royal family.

Eva happened to know a well-known media personality from Agona named Kwame Afrifa-Mensah, also known as Okatakyie Afrifa-Mensah.

Eva contacted him and he agreed to speak with me. I added him on Facebook and read a bit about him online. I noticed that he was also a chief and came across as a vibrant, outspoken individual.

I was able to have a conversation with Okatakyie Afrifa-Mensah after a few days. He was very welcoming on the phone and asked me to introduce myself properly since Eva had only mentioned me as her good friend without giving much information about me. I told him who I was and why I wanted to speak to him. He asked me why I was interested in finding out about my Agona Ashanti family and I explained that I had no idea I even had family there and was clueless about them until I did some research.

Okatakyie Afrifa-Mensah narrated a brief history of my great-great-grandfather, portraying him as a revered ruler and respected leader. He then asked if I comprehended the significance of knowing my royal family. I explained that it was crucial for understanding our identity and purpose on this earth. He confirmed he is also a member of my royal family and he advised me to make an effort to unite with them.

He confirmed my findings and encouraged me to visit Agona to pay homage to my royal heritage. I agreed to take him up on his suggestion and plan to visit the Agona traditional area in the future.

Overall, the research made me understand myself and my purpose in life. It's important to recognise and appreciate our strengths and qualities, such as bravery and determination, as they can help us overcome challenges and achieve our goals.

Having a sense of purpose can also be a powerful motivator in life; learning about my royal family history has helped me forge stronger connections with living family members and those I have never met.

It also helped me to discover distant cousins and uncover shared ancestors that I never knew existed.

I vow to continue on this journey of self-discovery and exploration of my family history because it can provide me with a deeper sense of purpose and direction in life.

Furthermore, by learning about my royal family lineage, I now can better understand the values, traditions and cultural practices that have been passed down through generations. This knowledge can help me connect with my heritage and identity on a deeper level.

In addition, this journey can also lead to new opportunities for family bonding and collaboration in the future for our generation. By sharing what I have learnt with my family members, we can all gain a better appreciation and understanding of our shared history and culture. This can foster a greater sense of unity and connectedness among us, as well as provide a platform for us to work together towards common goals.

Overall, this journey of self-discovery and exploration of my family history can be a transformative experience that helps me grow as an individual, connect with my heritage and strengthen the bonds with my family.

I decided to share my new findings with my auntie and explain why I thought it would be beneficial for our family to come together and rekindle our relationship with them. However, she didn't seem very enthusiastic about the idea of unity, but she did promise to give me her blessings if I ever wished to visit our royal family. While I was still curious about her reluctance to meet them, I chose not to press her further and respected her reasons.

Although there may have been underlying pain or issues, I am not certain why she was not happy with my findings. However, it is worth noting that she was not aware that her grandmother's father was enstooled three times. Despite her reaction, I believe that the research may have benefited her in some way.

I understand that some family history may have several potential consequences.

Family histories are often passed down through generations and can be subject to errors, exaggerations, and omissions. Sometimes, these stories are accepted as truth without fact-checking can lead to a distorted understanding of a family's past.

Family histories can be shaped by biases and prejudices that are not necessarily accurate or fair. Accepting these biases without question can perpetuate harmful stereotypes and perpetuate discrimination.

I also understand that by questioning my family's history, I may uncover previously unknown information or perspectives that can help me better understand my family's story and my own identity or have a bad effect on me which can lead to increased unresolved trauma.

Chapter 5
The New Chapter

Several months had passed, and I was eagerly anticipating the release of my first book, *The Unspoken Identity*. However, due to the Covid-19 pandemic outbreak, the publication of the book was significantly delayed. Finally, a release date of 30 November 2021, was scheduled.

I became ecstatic at the thought of becoming an official author, even though it was just an imagined feeling.

I promoted the upcoming book by spreading the news about its pre-order availability. To increase visibility, I also took pictures with prominent individuals who would help promote the book.

I informed everyone I came in contact with about my book.

Many people were shocked to learn that I had become a published author, particularly because I narrated my personal medical struggles in my book. Unfortunately, I also received some negative comments, with some questioning my motives and suggesting that I was seeking fame. These hurtful remarks were particularly disheartening, as they demonstrate a lack of understanding of the importance of advocacy.

I decided to take some measures to concentrate on my goals and not worry about what others think or say.

In order to build resilience and a strong spirit, it is important to focus on my personal growth and success. I knew it was not going to be easy to share my story or pursue my dreams, especially when others did not understand or support my choices. But ultimately, it is my life and my journey and only I have the power to shape it in the way that feels most authentic and fulfilling to me.

Without a doubt, everyone has different experiences and perspectives and not everyone will relate to or understand my choices. Whether they do or not, what is important is to stay true to myself and keep pushing towards my goals and visions even if it means stepping outside of my comfort zone and facing some criticism or scepticism from others.

My journey so far taught me to take steps towards my visions and goals by not allowing other people's opinions to hold me back. We all have the power to create the life we want and my story and journey are unique and valuable to me.

I dedicated all of my energy to promoting my book and taking every step necessary to ensure that it reaches as many people as possible.

I had a meeting with Her Excellency Rita Tani Iddi, the Deputy High Commissioner to the United Kingdom and Ireland, as well as Honourable Justin Frimpong Koduah, former Chief Executive Officer of the Youth Employment Agency in Ghana. Afterwards, I shared a signed copy with Councillor Margaret Greer, UNISON National Race Equality Officer and Labour Councillor for Lower Edmonton (UK), who had arranged the meeting. Meeting Cllr Margaret Greer again was delightful. She is an exemplary leader who inspires me greatly and it was a lovely opportunity to catch up with her.

I also arranged for a copy of the book to be delivered to Dr Samuel Iddrisu Seidu, a General Practitioner (GP) who happens to be one of my in-laws. In addition, I made sure that Sir Kwame Boakye Danquah, the Founder and President of Ghana Advocacy Group, received a signed copy, and influential personalities such as Councillor Maria Lovell, Former Mayor of Luton, CEO of The Ghana Society UK, and CEO of Miss Tourism Ghana UK, were also sent a copy.

Rev. Alexander Gyasi MBE, Senior Pastor of Highway of Holiness and CEO of Highway House Shelter arranged to take a copy and other influential personalities agreed to share it on their platforms to maximise sales and awareness.

The book had a significant impact, as it narrates my journey from childhood to the discovery of my reproductive health disorders. It portrays how I remained persistent and resilient in my quest for answers to my chronic pains, anxiety, recurrent infections and complications.

From the very first day of writing the book, I knew it would make waves and be accessible globally. I wanted to express my feelings and thoughts on why I decided to share my story with the world and also encourage other women to seek early medical intervention.

I believe my book is a stepping stone to create awareness about reproductive health disorders that people are not comfortable discussing.

When my book was finally released officially, I was overjoyed. The feeling of being an official author was indescribable. I felt like I had achieved a great accomplishment, especially by leaving a legacy and making my mother proud.

It was no surprise that I dedicated 'The Unspoken Identity' book to her.

My family and many others were excited for me and proud of my achievement. They encouraged me to continue making history. Within weeks of its release, I noticed that the book was available in reputable sources such as the British Library, Scribd and other major online retailers and academic platforms.

I decided to spend most of my time promoting the book, I begged friends to share the links to buy the book. I utilised every opportunity I got to promote the book.

Some friends were happy for me and congregated with me while some people became descents. Some stop picking up my calls or returning my calls.

It's not uncommon for some friends to change when they see you succeeding. While it can be hurtful or confusing, it's important to understand that there are a few reasons why this can happen.

I have noticed that when a person succeeds in something, it can often trigger feelings of jealousy or envy in others, especially if it is in the same area that a friend has been struggling with or trying to achieve. These feelings of envy can cause a rift in the friendship, as the friend may start to distance themselves or act differently towards the successful person.

Moreover, success often brings about changes in priorities and lifestyle. As an example, I have become increasingly busy with my advocacy work, social engagements, and other commitments.

I must admit that since embarking on this journey, I have had less time to spend with my friends and engage in activities that we used to enjoy together. This change in priorities may have caused a rift in most of my friendships and relationships.

However, I also expect my friends to understand that these changes in our friendships may be difficult to deal with. It is natural for people to change and grow apart over time. But once we all understand that life has changed, we can still surround ourselves with people who support and encourage our success.

I am extremely grateful to have friends like Amina, who understands my new life and busy schedule and still checks in on me from time to time. Whenever we have the chance, we make it a point to visit each other, even though it's not as often as before.

Amina frequently reaches out to check in on how my advocacy work is progressing and to inquire about my health challenges. During our conversations, we discuss a range of topics, including our personal lives, our families and the kind of things that close friends often discuss.

I am grateful to have a friend like Rachel in my life who is always there to support me and to offer assistance whenever I need it. She consistently donates to my NGO and goes above and beyond with her thoughtful gestures and caring demeanour. Rachel is truly a gem and I appreciate her kindness and friendship immensely.

Indeed, the life I have decided to embark upon is not an easy path. It is full of mysteries, unknown paths and great accomplishments. However, it requires me to stay grounded; stay focused, and avoid distractions. Success or breakthroughs do not happen in a day but through consistent work and commitment.

To stay on this path, I have to remind myself of my purpose and my goals regularly. I must be willing to put in the effort and stay committed even when it seems like nothing is happening. I know that every small step I take towards my goals will eventually lead to a breakthrough.

One thing that I have learnt on this journey is that distractions can be a significant hindrance to my success. Therefore, I have to learn to prioritise and manage my time effectively to achieve my objectives. This means that I must say no to certain things and be willing to make sacrifices in the short term to achieve my long-term goals which we all agree that it is not an easy task.

As I have decided to embark on this journey on this path, I must also learn to embrace failures and setbacks. They are not signs of weakness but rather opportunities for growth and improvement. Through failures, I can learn valuable lessons and become a better version of myself.

I understand that the path I have chosen may not be easy, but it is worth every effort. With consistency, commitment, focus and the right mindset, I know I can achieve my goals and fulfil my purpose.

It is common to struggle with saying 'no' to friends or prioritising personal goals when we care deeply about our relationships with others. I learnt it was important to remember that while supporting friends is a valuable aspect of any friendship, it is also essential to take care of myself and my own well-being. I know setting boundaries can be challenging, but I felt it was an important skill to learn for my own mental and emotional health.

Also, evaluating my priorities and goals became crucial to me. I started to take some time to reflect on what is most important to me in life and what I need to do to achieve those goals. This method has helped me establish boundaries and prioritise my time and energy accordingly.

I noticed that the more I practised saying 'no' in a respectful and compassionate way was very important in any relationship. I have learnt to express appreciation for a friend's request, but also explain that not every request I can be able to fulfil at a particular time. Surely, setting boundaries and prioritising my own needs is not selfish. It's essential for my own well-being and allows me to be a better friend in the long run.

Throughout my journey, I have learnt to focus on building new relationships with people who share my values and goals. I have also come to realise that it's okay to let go of friendships that no longer serve me.

I feel certain that my book publication is a great accomplishment of which I am proud.

But I continued to have doubts and insecurities, even when I knew I had achieved the great things I had worked hard for.

I was still feeling sad and questioned whether I was on the right path. I failed to acknowledge those feelings and understand where they came from.

What made me sadder sometimes was when I experienced rejection from sponsors or people who refused to donate towards the Speciallady Awareness cause, and this was discouraging sometimes.

But I learnt that not everyone will understand or support Speciallady Awareness's vision or mission. Besides, I can't control other people's actions, but can only control my own.

And the more I realised this I kept pushing forward and spreading awareness of reproductive health disorders.

I have always believed that eventually, I will find the right support.

As for being 'The Special Lady', I can feel deep inside me that is my true calling, although, the predicament sometimes makes me question myself.

But when I reflect on the good works Speciallady Awareness have done so far, I become very happy and fulfilled. I observed that there were some frustrating events or incidents, I kept experiencing in this advocacy work.

It is unfortunate that some people engage in unnecessary competition even in the context of charitable work. And it is clear everyone has their own motivations and insecurities and sometimes those can lead to unhealthy behaviours such as trying to undermine or outdo others.

I ensured that I did not allow those negative experiences to overshadow the positive impact I was making through my charitable work.

I kept focusing on the reasons why I got involved in the first place and the people I was helping.

I tried my best to surround myself with supportive individuals who genuinely wanted to see me succeed and grow. I also focus on the positive aspects of the work. Raising awareness and advocating for reproductive health disorders bring joy and a sense of purpose as many women and young girls are being inspired.

Discovery

As 2021 draws to an end, I find myself eagerly anticipating the opportunities that the year 2022 will bring. One of my major goals for the coming year was to launch my book in both the UK and Ghana, which was an exciting prospect. Additionally, my NGO, Speciallady Awareness, had several projects planned for 2022, which I was looking forward to coordinating.

However, I cannot ignore the financial constraints that my organisation faced throughout the years 2020 and 2021. These limitations made it difficult for us to engage in the outreach activities that are essential to achieving our mission. Despite the challenges that we faced, I remained determined to ensure that we continued to make progress towards our goals in the coming year.

As I reflected on the year 2021, I admitted that the year 2021 has been one of the most stressful periods for me and my team. Nevertheless, I was confident that with dedication and perseverance, we will be able to overcome these obstacles and achieve great things in the New Year (2022).

My family and I had decided to spend the Christmas holidays with my sister and her family. We had planned many activities for the children, such as going to Winter Wonderland and shopping, as well as preparing lots of food for everyone. We started celebrating the festive season before the actual day of Christmas and even received some family members from Ghana.

However, just a couple of days before Christmas, the family members who came from Ghana were diagnosed with Covid-19. In response, we all decided to get tested for Covid-19 and some of us received negative results while others tested positive. We continued to isolate ourselves and as a result, Christmas day was not as joyful as we had planned. Unfortunately, we could not have the proper Christmas dinner that we had anticipated due to the circumstances.

On Boxing Day, I decided to return home with my family. While my husband was driving us back, I started feeling unwell and I immediately knew that I had contracted the Covid-19 virus. I became worried, especially because I knew my immune system was not the best when it came to battling infections or illnesses.

As soon as we arrived home, I got a test kit and my daughter, husband and I all took the test. They both tested negative, while I tested positive. I then started to isolate, which was awful and one of the loneliest times of the year. It was challenging to live in the same household with people yet not be able to hug or have conversations with them or be close to them. The fact that the affected person had to wear a mask and avoid mingling with the rest of the household only added to the difficulty.

I started using steam, applying vapour rub on my chest and back, drinking hot herbal teas and soups and chewing ginger with honey to minimise my Covid-19 symptoms. Despite these efforts, I was constantly coughing and experiencing high fever and body pains. Unfortunately, a few days after my diagnosis, my daughter also tested positive for the virus.

I was devastated because I did not want her to experience the same pain that I was going through and I did not want her to miss out on her education. However, this circumstance was beyond my control.

Despite my worries, when my daughter, Rashley, contracted Covid-19, she remained surprisingly strong. She continued to eat, acted normally and played around, while I was struggling with severe symptoms. Watching her remain resilient was a relief amidst a difficult situation.

She had to attend her class through online tutorials and she enjoyed being at home with me while we both treated our illness symptoms. She tested negative after about five days, while it took me a good two weeks to get a negative test result. It took me almost one month to regain my energy and my menstrual cycle became very irregular.

Furthermore, my back pains remained excruciating, causing me constant worry as my gynaecological condition's symptoms worsened. Despite having received all the Covid-19 vaccinations, contracting the virus severely exacerbated my known gynaecological conditions. As a patient with bowel endometriosis, adhesions, multiple fibroids and uterus didelphys, I often experience a plethora of symptoms. Although I was no more under the hospital's obstetrics and gynaecology care for nearly a year, it appeared that the Covid-19 virus triggered my chronic pains and fatigue. I was quite worried when my doctor decided to carry out some blood tests and scans, and possibly refer me back to the specialist.

In November, I received a message from the BBC Africa or BBC Pidgin team. They had expressed interest in carrying out a documentary about my story after seeing my interview at Ghana Broadcasting Corporation in October 2021. I was thrilled about this opportunity and we had several productive discussions about my availability and the documentary itself.

We finally conducted the documentary.

In March 2022, the documentary that I worked on with BBC Pidgin and BBC Africa was released.

When the documentary was released in many countries in Africa, it was a huge success and it had a significant impact on the world by spreading the importance of speaking up and seeking early medical intervention, raising awareness about rare congenital abnormalities and being able to inspire others on a global scale.

My previous documentary with Born Different Shows was not released in most African countries although, while it was a huge success, it was released mostly in Europe, Asia, Canada etc.

Therefore, I rejoiced when I realised this opportunity was going to help me reach a wider audience as Born Different Shows.

Sharing my story with BBC Africa and BBC Pidgin was released to many African countries. This opportunity ensured that my story reached a vast and diverse audience, which was able to help create a broader awareness of reproductive health issues. This broad reach also helped in generating a global conversation on the rare biological abnormality of uterus didelphys (two wombs, two cervixes and two vaginal canals) which led to a more significant impact and change.

The documentary definitely was a powerful tool for shaping public opinion and raising awareness on unspoken topics such as menstrual hygiene and reproductive health overall.

I believe my story and journey could reach policymakers and decision-makers worldwide, thereby increasing the likelihood of change in women's reproductive health and combating menstrual poverty.

I strongly believe that my story could serve as a means of creating communication surrounding reproductive health and awareness of menstrual health and hygiene.

One of the reasons why I agreed to share my story with BBC Africa and BBC Pidgin was to set a pathway to opportunities for funding and support from different organisations, governments and individuals. I knew this opportunity can sometimes increase financial support which can help in creating more impactful and lead to greater awareness and change.

Certainly, my documentary will have a long-term impact on society by creating a lasting legacy of awareness and change.

Coming from an African background, topics relating to reproductive health and menstruation are rarely discussed. Therefore, reaching a broad audience can inspire people to take action and make positive changes in their communities and beyond.

Undoubtedly, the release of my documentary in multiple countries had a powerful impact on the world by raising awareness and shaping public opinion. When my story was first released in 2019 by Born Different Shows, I received backlash from many people, which made me realise that more awareness was needed. That's why I decided to write my first book and continue to work towards sustainable change in reproductive health and combat menstrual poverty through Speciallady Awareness initiatives.

Since I could not be present at the Wiamoase Library and Conference Centre Grande opening, I delegated my team from my NGO m Rashly to donate six hundred and fifty books to the newly built ultra-modern library and conference centre.

I thought that donating books would be beneficial for the children and young adults who frequent the library, and I was appreciative when two UK libraries provided me with book donations. Additionally, I purchased a significant number of books from charity shops in order to expand the quantity of books available for donation.

I also organised a small party to feed over two hundred orphans and donated toys and essentials in April 2022.

I have always believed that donating to orphans is a noble cause as it has a significant positive impact on the lives of vulnerable children who have lost their parents or guardians. It is unfortunate but true that many orphans lack basic necessities such as food, shelter, clothing and healthcare. This is why donating to support these children is crucial in providing them with the essentials they need to survive and thrive.

Furthermore, a lack of education and opportunities to learn can impede their future dreams and aspirations. This is why I choose to donate to provide them with the necessary resources to attend school and receive an education that can change their lives. I often donate educational materials and cover their school fees to give them this opportunity.

I believe that by providing them with access to education, they can achieve their goals, unlock their potential and ultimately experience greater success and financial stability.

Many vulnerable children require emotional support, as they have lost their parents or those responsible for their care. This trauma can lead to long-term psychological effects and in some cases, even drive them to take tragic measures that can have negative consequences on their lives.

While there are many agencies in Ghana that take care of such children, it appears that many still lack access to basic healthcare and life essentials. Investing in these children's lives can help them break the cycle of poverty and provide them with hope for a better future.

I often provide mentoring sessions for some of these children to help build their self-esteem and confidence. Due to their childhood experiences and past traumas, they often need a positive role model or someone they can look up to. While I cannot fully understand their unique situations, I empathise with them as I have also experienced the loss of a mother.

Supporting these children brings me a sense of fulfilment and purpose, knowing that I am contributing to the development of our planet. It is heart-breaking to see how many people still lack basic necessities in life. However, by donating our time, resources and services, we can make a positive difference and improve the lives of those in need. Knowing that we are making a tangible impact and touching the lives of others is a truly rewarding and meaningful experience.

It is my dream to achieve extreme financial success so that I can help people who lack access to financial breakthroughs. Whenever I visit rural areas in Ghana and meet people who can barely afford a daily meal, it breaks my heart. I am fortunate to live in a country where I can afford to eat daily, access healthcare services and receive education. However, there are many individuals in countries like Ghana who struggle financially. Unlike in Western countries, Ghana lacks a government support system that could finance or support young people to engage in ventures or activities to generate income for the youth.

Hence, it is a collective responsibility for government officials, agencies and individuals to join together and support young people and people who lack access to financial breakthroughs.

Chapter 6
The Journey of Self-Transformation

February 2022 was a delightful period as Speciallady Awareness celebrated its fifth anniversary. Looking back, the NGO carried out outreach activities in fifteen schools and donated medical supplies and sanitary products worth thousands of pounds to communities, hospitals, and schools in Ghana. These donations supported essential medical care for women with reproductive health issues and helped combat menstrual poverty.

Recalling all the wonderful work that my NGO has done, I must admit that I was proud and grateful for every effort that I have put in to achieve these excellent results.

Initially, I had planned to launch my book in April 2022. However, I changed my mind and instead decided to invest in the London Book Fair. This turned out to be a marvellous opportunity for me, as my book was going to be showcased there.

When I visited the two-day show, it was an amazing experience. Seeing my book on shelves and exposed to thousands of guests, publishers and other industry professionals was overwhelming. As I entered the auditorium, I was struck by the banners, press, well-known publishers and even some celebrities. I couldn't believe my book was on display.

To find my book, I consulted the map and navigated my way around the show. There were so many activities on offer, including talks on publishing, writing books, marketing and even arts and dancing. Overall, it was a truly unforgettable experience.

A week after attending the London Book Fair, I began working at Wealthtime Limited, a company that specialises in pensions and investments. It was been an excellent firm to work for, and I felt fortunate to have joined their team.

Within just a few weeks of working for the company, I had the honour of being featured in the company newsletter. Additionally, one of my directors purchased copies of my book to distribute to the staff. This gesture made me feel incredibly appreciated and it was heartening to see that they were interested in my advocacy work and extracurricular activities outside of work.

Overall, I felt grateful to be part of such a supportive and encouraging work environment and I was excited to continue contributing to the company's success.

After meeting my supervisor, Natalie, I felt as though I had known her for years. She was incredibly down to earth and always checked in on me. Her calm and gentle demeanour was truly lovely to see.

In June 2022, I had the pleasure of being invited to Buckingham Palace for the Commonwealth reception and I was ecstatic to meet King Charles (who was the Prince of Wales at the time). I vividly remember receiving a phone call from Mrs Freda Bediako-Puni, a Minister Counsellor for the Republic of Ghana who is the head of Commonwealth & Diaspora affairs. She requested my details to be sent to Buckingham Palace as I had been nominated as a guest to the Commonwealth reception. I felt extremely grateful for this opportunity and eagerly looked forward to the occasion. Mrs Bediako-Puni explained that the ceremony was to celebrate the Commonwealth Diaspora of the United Kingdom.

I was pleasantly surprised to discover that I was nominated as one of the most influential Ghanaian personalities in the UK. It was an honour to be considered alongside so many accomplished individuals. I believed that my work may have inspired others and I was grateful that Ghanaian leaders recognised my efforts.

As a person, it is natural to question rewards and recognition, especially when I think back on how I started my advocacy work and how far I have come in sharing my story.

Every day feels like a learning curve and a journey for me. Doubts, setbacks and trials along the way made me question whether I was on the right path. However, when I received the invitation to meet with the UK Royal Family and recalled all the awards and recommendations I have received, these experiences made me feel incredibly appreciated and fulfilled.

Being recognised and receiving awards or recommendations is a wonderful feeling of validation and appreciation for my hard work and dedication. This recognition made me realise that not only was my work acknowledged, but I was also recognised as an individual who has achieved something meaningful. Such recognition serves as a source of motivation, inspiring me to continue striving towards excellence in all aspects of my life.

The reception was hosted by their Royal Highnesses The Prince of Wales and The Duchess of Cornwall on Thursday 9 June 2022. There were going to be representatives from all fifty-four Commonwealth countries attending.

Just a couple of days before the Commonwealth reception, I received a call from Tim, a member of my Rotary Club, informing me that the club's executive wanted to schedule a meeting with me. I felt a sense of fear and concern, wondering if I had violated any of Rotary's rules or standards for being a Rotarian.

The meeting was scheduled and on the day of the meeting, one of the executives began by expressing their pride in me for promoting the work of Rotary International in Great Britain and Ireland and for advocating for the impact of our work. They praised my efforts and dedication to the organisation.

Rotary Global Hub was established during Covid-19 pandemic period and it became the fastest-growing Rotary International club in the world.

The Rotary Global Hub aimed to bring people together in a purpose-built online environment to work towards making a difference in communities around the world.

During the meeting, Tim spoke highly of my work and its alignment with the vision of Rotary Global Hub and Rotary International as a whole. He emphasised that my advocacy for reproductive health had been an inspiration to many women despite the challenges posed by my rare congenital abnormality and medical complications. I was thrilled to hear such kind words and to know that I have broken taboos and become a voice for women and girls suffering from gynaecological conditions.

Although I was overjoyed with the compliments I received, I was really surprised when I was given the honour to serve as president. Not only had I been new to Rotary for only one year, but I also felt that I needed more experience, skills and knowledge to lead effectively. However, they made me realise that my consistent work and advocacy clearly demonstrated my abilities as an outstanding leader and they would guide me throughout my journey.

I suppose my role as president of Rotary Global Hub will prove that Rotary International is a modern, vibrant, flexible, innovative and inclusive organisation.

I was delighted to be given the chance to prove to communities that I can lead.

I presumed that I could bring on board the skills, accomplishments and knowledge I have acquired from my experience as a founder of an NGO, my diverse work experience and my educational background to be an outstanding leader at Rotary Global Hub. I know I have the ability to inspire, motivate and guide others towards a common goal as seen in most of the projects my NGO have done to promote reproductive health rights among women and young girls.

I knew I had a clear vision of where an organisation want to go or achieve hence why I believe this opportunity helped me to communicate this vision to other Rotarians in a way that inspires and motivates them to promote Rotary International initiatives.

Being the president made me an excellent communicator as it improved my listening skills and helped me communicate effectively ideas and visions.

As a leader, I knew I had the ability to put myself in other people's shoes and understand their perspectives and feelings. This skill aided me in building strong relationships with other members of the Rotary Global Hub and other Rotary clubs.

The position made me improve my personality and I became more honest, ethical and trustworthy which helped me in other areas of my life.

I was able to adapt to the change of being a president, running an NGO and being a mentor to other youth. Hence, I was good at handling unexpected situations with ease. I became more resilient and good at dealing with difficult situations.

Then I was able to bounce back from setbacks and failures. This position gave me a growth mindset and I was constantly learning and improving.

It also encourages some people and inspires them to be focused and work towards success.

The day of the Commonwealth reception finally arrived and I chose to wear a beautiful long green and white floral dress that flattered my body. I paired it with medium black heels, light makeup and minimal jewellery.

The colours of my dress symbolise beginnings and growth, renewal, abundance and a sense of calm and balance. I strive to embody these qualities in my daily life, along with fearlessness, optimism, independence and a strong opinion.

As I stepped out of the cab and made my way towards the entrance of Buckingham Palace, I was struck by the beauty of the architectural building and the grandeur of the palace.

There were numerous security staff guarding the premises and controlling entry into the palace.

As I approached the entrance, I had the opportunity to meet and converse with other invited guests. We discussed our respective professions and exchanged contact information, making plans to stay in touch after the ceremony. It was a great opportunity to network with like-minded individuals and make valuable connections.

After our invitations and belongings were checked and searched, we proceeded to the main entrance of the palace. As we walked through the stunning architectural building, I could not help but admire every aspect of it while engaging in conversations with other invited guests. It was surreal to find myself in the company of distinguished figures from various Commonwealth communities, as well as humanitarians and leaders.

I was amazed to be considered one of the great influential personalities among them.

This reception made me realise that I had to continue to work towards sustainable change and grow in the world around me.

I comprehended that consistent work is key to achieving great outcomes in any area of life. Consistency helps build momentum. By working consistently, I knew it would result in working towards a goal every day or every week.

I know I shall develop a routine and a sense of purpose that can keep me motivated and on track. The more I work consistently, it can be helpful when I encounter obstacles or setbacks, as it will give me the resilience to keep pushing forward.

Another benefit of consistent work is that it allows me to build skills and knowledge over time. When I practice a skill or learn something new on a regular basis, it will deepen my understanding and become more proficient. This can lead to improved performance, increased confidence and more opportunities for growth and advancement.

Indeed, consistent work can also help me to develop a sense of discipline and focus. I knew prioritising my goals and commitment as well as working towards them consistently, will certainly help me to develop habits that support my success. Working consistently helps me to shut out distractions and set goals while keeping me on track towards my success.

Additionally, consistent work is a powerful tool for achieving great outcomes. Whether in my personal or professional life, consistent hard work is very important.

Committing to consistent effort over time can help me build momentum, develop skills and knowledge and cultivate discipline and focus. I strongly believe that my consistent efforts, hard work and prayers have brought me this far.

Having had the privilege to meet the royal family and participate in such a remarkable occasion, my mind was filled with the realisation that my philanthropic work had brought me to this point and enabled me to achieve extraordinary things.

I was fortunate enough to receive recognition from various award bodies in the UK and Ghana for my philanthropic work. As I received more awards, I found that more doors and opportunities began to open up for me.

Difficult Times Create Growth

I decided to launch my book in Ghana and use the funds raised from the launch to promote reproductive health rights and combat menstrual poverty. To help achieve this, I reached out to a family friend who is also a Rotarian and an executive member of the Rotary Club of Kumasi, Nana Effah. He agreed to speak to his club to collaborate with my NGO, S Speciallady Awareness, about our cause.

Rotary Club of Kumasi graciously agreed to partner with Speciallady Awareness, and my patron and the Special Lady Awareness trustees were all involved in organising the book launch. They used their networks to invite their contacts and I personally sent invitations to prominent people in Ghana. I was expecting 150 guests to attend.

Initially, preparations for the event were going smoothly and most of my invited guests had agreed to attend. However, the costs involved in the preparations began to exceed the budget that had been set at the outset. Adding to the financial strain was the depreciation of the Ghanaian currency, the cedi, which led to an increase in local inflation and made imports more expensive. Ghanaian importers were finding it challenging to stay afloat due to the high cost of importing and clearing goods from local ports. As a result, the cost of goods and services rose significantly.

The price of the venue and services we enquire prior to organising the book launch changed dramatically every week.

I started facing some challenges with people who pledged to support our project financially, as they did not fulfil their pledges. Also, some who volunteered to promote our project prior to its launch became distant. This caused tension to rise among the team.

As the weeks and months went by, I noticed that some of the people I relied on had started to disappoint me. They stopped answering my calls, emails, or messages, which made me, panic and consider withdrawing from the book launch.

However, this behaviour was unusual for me when it came to Speciallady Awareness initiatives. Instead of giving up, I usually persist and find ways to accomplish every task that is set up.

I discerned that it was important not to quit a dream or task for many right reasons. Firstly for my personal growth, it is clear that pursuing a dream or task requires effort, perseverance and commitment, which can help me to develop resilience, discipline and self-confidence. Whether I was able to accomplish the task or not at least, I would have learnt some valuable lessons which would be useful for other areas of my life or in the future.

I believe that pursuing a task that is meaningful to me could bring a sense of purpose and fulfilment to my life, which was exactly the reason why I decided to raise funds and awareness to promote reproductive health rights among women and young girls in Ghana.

I believed that launching the book was a way of making a positive difference in the world and it was going to give me a sense of pride and accomplishment.

Also due to the fact that I invited prominent individuals, it was definitely going to bring opportunities such as networking, future collaborations, meeting new people, learning new skills, or discovering new passions that can lead myself and other members of Special Lady Awareness NGO as well as the invited.

To be frank, the difficulties and challenges I was facing were causing me sleepless nights. In an attempt to distract myself from the problems of the world, I was pouring all my focus into the book launch.

During the same year, my husband was deployed to Estonia. Since 2017, the UK normally sends an armoured battle group consisting of Challenger 2 tanks and Warrior infantry fighting vehicles to Estonia. The group normally has around 800 to 900 personnel and is on a rotating six-month tour.

Since February 2023, the British Army presence in Estonia doubled, with numbers continuing to increase. As a result, my husband was one of the service personnel who were deployed to Estonia.

With Russia's invasion and occupation of parts of Ukraine, tensions escalated in the Russo-Ukrainian War. As a result, my worry has continued to increase, especially considering the fact that my husband was currently in Estonia.

I am aware military wives are among the strongest and most resilient women in the world. As we face unique challenges and sacrifices that require immense strength, courage and determination to overcome.

As a military wife myself, I understand the challenges of enduring long periods of separation from our loved ones when our spouses are away serving in another country. During these times, I have had to manage the household, raise my daughter and deal with the daily stresses of life on my own. But the experience with my husband's deployment to Estonia was another emotional episode, especially since my daughter was old enough to ask questions about Ukraine and why her father had to be away. I continued to reassure her that her father was safe and that we should pray for him always.

I was struggling with constant fear and uncertainty surrounding the potential outcome of a Russian invasion of Estonia. Despite these challenges, I knew that I had unwavering strength and support. I know I have always stood by my husband through thick and thin, offering encouragement when he needed it the most. My priority has always been to provide a strong foundation for my family, creating a sense of stability and security that helps our daughter cope with the challenges of military life.

As an army spouse, it is important for me to always play an active role in supporting my husband. During the invasion of Ukraine, I was contacted by the National Union of Ghanaian Students Association UK (NUGSA UK) President Mr Lord Mc Mensah as I was one of their volunteer members of the Welfare Committee.

They asked me to help evacuate students who were stuck in Ukraine. While some of them were able to leave Ukraine and reach neighbouring countries, there were still hundreds of students who remained stuck in Ukraine and needed assistance.

I was deeply moved and concerned about the tragedies happening to the students, so I joined the committee to help keep them safe. I stayed in constant communication with the students. The committee focused on different parts of Ukraine and Sumy was one of the cities I was providing support to.

On a daily basis, I was checking on how they were coping and trying to assist them in finding food and other essentials.

I contacted many organisations but with the density of the bombing and safety issues, it was really difficult for organisations to easily enter Sumy to rescue or give support to the students.

I contacted many organisations, but due to the high density of the bombing and safety concerns, it was challenging for them to provide immediate rescue or support to the students in Sumy.

Additionally, I played a role in getting Ghanaian government officials involved to help ensure their safe departure from Ukraine. It was always terrifying to hear the sounds of bombs and see the students scrambling to hide under tunnels during attacks.

The fact that my husband was deployed nearby gave me added bravery to help with the rescue of the students.

It was a great relief when the students were successfully rescued and taken to neighbouring countries for safety. Some of the students kept in touch with me and we communicated regularly to ensure that they had settled well in their new surroundings.

I have always loved volunteering and being involved in various community works, such as organising events, fundraising and providing free mentoring sessions. These activities have given me strength, courage and resilience in the face of adversity. Through them, I learn something new every day and continue to grow as a person.

Volunteering has taught me the value of persistence in pursuing my dreams and goals. Life's challenges and experiences can easily become limitations, but by staying focused and determined, I have learnt to overcome them. Overall, my volunteer experiences have had a positive impact on my personal and professional development.

This is why I am proud to be a Rotarian as I can easily work with like-minded individuals who believe in changing the world in a positive way and making an impact.

With only a few weeks left until the launch of my book, *The Unspoken Identity*, I was feeling the pressure and experiencing a lot of stress and disappointment. I confided in Eva about my struggles and she introduced me to some of her contacts. Although I was considering postponing the book launch, I did not want to delay it because the scheduled date was 10 November 2022. Additionally, the one-year anniversary of the book's publication would be on 30 November, so it was important to launch it on time. Furthermore, I was not able to launch the book in April in the UK, so it was even more crucial to stick to the November date.

She told her friend, Nana Kumi Kodie I, was going to do his best to assist me. He pledged to support my book launch by providing ushers, security personnel and Adowa dancers to grace the occasion. Adowa dancers are Ghanaian dancers who use hand and foot movements to express their emotions and feelings, and there are different hand movements performed for each occasion. So, the dancers will communicate positive emotions and happiness through their dance performance during the book launch.

This ceremony felt very prestigious and I was grateful for the support Nana Kumi Kodie was giving me. However, it seemed that the more effort I put into preparing for the book launch, the more I needed to spend on other services and goods. At this point, I had exceeded my budget, but my main goal was to raise enough funds to support women who were struggling with gynaecological conditions and menstrual poverty. After discussing this with Nana Kumi Kodie, he suggested that I also auction off some paintings alongside the books.

This was a brilliant idea; however, at the time, I was not aware of any artists in Ghana who would be willing to donate their artworks for the auction. Nevertheless, I was determined to make it happen and promised to reach out to someone I knew who creates amazing artwork. I enquired a few people but there was no positive response.

After a few weeks, Nana Kumi introduced Samuel, the CEO of Affluent Art and he sent me some of his works. I was blown away by their quality and asked him if he was sure he wanted to donate his work for the book launch. Samuel agreed and I decided to offer him a percentage of the proceeds after the auction as compensation for his time and materials.

Some of the guests invited to the book launch included representatives from Ghana Health Services, such as Programme Manager Mr Michael Ige from the United Nations Population Fund (UNFPA) Ghana. Also in attendance were Akwamu Traditional Area Paramount Chief Odeneho Kwafo Akoto III, the Paramount Queen Mother Nana Afrakoma II, officials from Ghana Social Welfare, Ghana Library Authority CEO Hayford Siaw and many others.

A few weeks prior to the book launch, my friend Jeremiah introduced me to Mr Hayford Siaw, the CEO of Ghana Library Authority. I contacted Mr Siaw and requested to send a copy of my book to donate to the library. However, he pointed out that the book had to be evaluated to determine whether it met the criteria for inclusion in the Ghana Library Authority catalogue. I reassured him that I believed it did meet the criteria since the book was already available on

Scribd, the largest digital library in the world and was also accessible via WorldCat, Portico Archive and various academic resources.

He gave me his office address for me to send the book. I prayed fervently for a miracle to happen so that the Ghana Library Authority would accept the book before the launch date. After he received the book, he asked me to wait while they assessed it. Every couple of days, I grew increasingly impatient and contacted him to check on the progress.

With just a week left before the book launch, the Ghana Library Authority confirmed that they had accepted the book and it would be accessible through their library catalogue.

This was another milestone for the book. However, upon learning of this good news, I could not help but wonder why I hadn't experienced a financial breakthrough with the sales of the book. Yet, as I reflected on the book's reach and the various academic resources it had garnered, I could not be ungrateful. Instead, I continued to thank God for such favour.

Chapter 7
Outdooring

As the speakers for the book launch confirmed their attendance, I was filled with excitement and disbelief that such influential personalities had agreed to speak at the event. Finally, on Thursday, 10 November 2022, the day of the book launch arrived and I was quite nervous.

To ensure that I was on time for the launch, I had spent the previous night at the Airport West Hotel. The night seemed never-ending as I prepared for the launch with Miriam, who had been an invaluable help throughout the planning process. She had made sure that all the necessary items, paintings, gift bags and hampers were adequately prepared for the event.

We had breakfast in the morning, but I could not hide my nerves, even though I tried to act normal. Deep down, I was praying that all the guests, special guests and speakers would attend and that the book launch would be a success. Looking out of the hotel restaurant's windows, the sun was shining and it felt like a warm early morning. I had an appointment to get my nails and pedicure done, so I quickly called for a cab and headed to the salon to get myself glammed up. At the salon, I asked the beauticians to hurry so that I could make it to my makeup appointment at the hotel at 11 a.m. As they worked on my nails, I kept changing the colours and could not make up my mind.

As I sat in the salon chair, the time seemed to pass quickly. Before I knew it, the beauticians had finished my nails and pedicure. I requested a cab and returned to my hotel, which was just a five-minute drive away.

As I got into the cab, I realised that I wanted to buy some water and a drink to celebrate after the book launch. Perhaps my nervousness was causing me to think of distractions. I quickly stopped at the supermarket and was in and out in less than 15 minutes. Then, I headed back to the hotel to prepare for the launch.

Upon my arrival at the hotel, my makeup artist and her team promptly arrived with all their equipment, including makeup chairs, lights, sets, kits and various other items. After settling into the makeup high chair, I requested a light and elegant makeup look and asked them not to take too much time as I still needed to be styled for the upcoming event.

I went downstairs and saw the decorators and hotel staff setting up the hall for the launch. They asked me to go back upstairs and leave everything to them since it was their job. I started to wonder if they had everything they needed for the setup and whether I was needed to assist them. They must have noticed that I was becoming nervous, so they reassured me that everything was under control and I should not worry. They advised me to focus on getting myself ready for the event instead.

I returned to my hotel room.

As I sat for my makeup application, I received a series of messages from attendees confirming their attendance, while others noted they would be sending representatives instead.

I was panicking and praying for a successful book launch when my mentee, Princess Wedaga, knocked on my hotel room door. She entered with a huge smile and said, "Congratulations!" I smiled back and replied that we hope for the best.

Wedaga is an incredible mentee and any mentor would be lucky to work with her. She always calls me 'mummy' and confides in me about her career, personal life and life goals. It is an extraordinary feeling to have so many young ladies looking up to me and seeing me as their role model.

At around 2 p.m., I made my way to the hotel conference hall where the book launch was being held. Upon arriving, I saw that many of the guests had already taken their seats. The ushers kindly greeted me and showed me to my seat at the front of the room, where I smiled at the crowd.

Once I had taken my seat, my fellow speakers joined me. They reassured me that we were well-prepared for the event and congratulated me with warm smiles.

The MCs for the launch, Prince Prempeh, Past President of the Rotary Club of Kumasi and Mz Gee, a renowned Ghanaian media personality, journalist and broadcaster, welcomed the guests and began the programme. They introduced the book launch and the reason why gathered.

They explained that each speaker would be introduced according to their scheduled speaking slot.

I was thrilled as the special guests were introduced and honoured their invitation to attend the launch. As I watched them take their seats, I started to feel more relaxed and confident that the day would go well.

During the event, Dr Abena Okoh, Director of the Accra Metro Health Directorate (Ghana Health Services), was the first speaker. She emphasised the importance of creating a safe space for women to openly discuss their reproductive and sexual health. Dr Okoh encouraged all agencies and individuals to promote reproductive health rights and applauded the initiative taken to raise awareness of gynaecological conditions and menstrual health and hygiene. Furthermore, she commended you for your efforts in this area.

During the event, one of the speakers Dr Pinaman Appau, a Hospital Director & Consultant Psychiatrist and Hospital Director at the Accra Psychiatric Hospital, delivered a keynote speech. Dr Appau is also a Diversity, Equity and Inclusion Specialist and Researcher and she is Ghana's first female Psychiatrist trained by the Ghana College of Physicians and Surgeons. Over the past fifteen years, she has worked tirelessly to improve mental health across several regions of the country.

In her keynote speech, Dr Appau emphasised the importance of mental health awareness and urged patients to seek early diagnosis and treatment or therapies. Her message underscored the crucial role of early intervention in preventing mental health issues from escalating.

As the MC introduced my biography and praised me for writing *The Unspoken Identity* book, I realised that the task had finally been accomplished. I was the third speaker and I presented my speech, explaining why I chose to write my story in the form of a book. I urged the audience to help me raise awareness and funds to support women's reproductive health and combat menstrual poverty.

My speech was short and to the point and I delivered it with clarity and confidence. I spoke without any noticeable mistakes; my tone was clear and articulated.

Nana Esi, Deputy Commissioner at Ghana Revenue Authority and a member of the Institute of Chartered Accountants Ghana and the Chartered Institute of Taxation was the following speaker after my speech.

She is well-versed in risk management techniques and has been working with the Ghana Revenue Authority for more than twenty years. After serving as the first female tax audit head in the northern sector. Nana Esi is a two-time past President of the Rotary Club of Kumasi.

During her speech, she added the importance of sexual education and prevention of teenage pregnancy, STI, etc.

The final speaker was Vanessa Mensah-Kabu, who is a medical Doctor at the West African Rescue Association.

Dr Vanessa is an advocate for Health, Gender Equity, Women and Girl Child Empowerment. Dr Vanessa is known for her advocacy, her passion and her drive to ensure health is understood by everyone through education and by creating awareness through various outreach projects and media platforms for many years. Dr Vanessa Mensah-Kabu educated the audience on the understanding of rare congenital abnormalities and other reproductive health disorders.

She explained how these conditions could affect women's lifestyles, relationships, career goals, etc.

She stated how medical practitioners should ensure that essential medical care is given to patients who exhibit symptoms and signs of reproductive health disorders.

Some of my good friends who attended were Justin Duah and Nana Yaw Acheampong from Operations from the office of the president of the Republic of Ghana and Mr Richard Gyamfi Head of International Relations at Ghana Scholarship Secretariat, Amb. Ashim Morton, the President of Millennium Excellence Foundation, Honourable Ras Mubarak, A renowned Ghanaian media personality Yaw Ampofo Ankrah, Roselyn Felli TV Presenter, NPP UK Branch Chairman Mr Kingsley Adumattah Agyapong, Oseadeeyo Nana Kumi Kodie I, Hemaa Adwoa Enyinfuaa III, Derek Nyarko President of Rotary Club of Kumasi, Dr Marzuq from the Office of National Chief Imam, Nana Effah Mensah Director of Projects at Rotary Club of Kumasi, Sarfoa Asamoah Ghana Most Beautiful Winner 2021, Wedaga Ghana Most Beautiful third runner up & Miss Heritage World 2022 beauty with purpose and many other personalities were present at the book launch.

Speciallady Awareness Trustee Hajia Salima Iddrisu Former Deputy Director for Social Welfare and Emelia Sackey came to support.

I met Emelia Sackey at a conference and we hit it off straight away. We had an instant connection and it felt like we had known each other for years.

She hugely supported my book launch.

My friends Victory Quaye and Mawu Dola were very supportive and helpful to me during my book launch.

The book launch was a resounding success, with guests generously donating funds and purchasing paintings at a reasonable price. The conference hall we used at the Airport West Hotel was beautifully decorated and the hospitality was outstanding. The staff were highly professional and the quality of service they delivered was exceptional, which made a lasting impression on everyone who attended the event.

After the launch, I received numerous messages of congratulations. When the book launch was featured in newspapers and online news platforms, people reached out to commend me. I was amazed by the success of the event.

There were four bloggers, three photographers and two videographers present at the launch.

Security personnel were also present and there were eight ushers. Samuel, the CEO of Affluent Art, was given a platform to explain the concepts behind his paintings. He was thrilled to have such an opportunity.

I was overjoyed and grateful when we raised a significant amount of funds for the cause.

Over the next few days, I dedicated my time to the Speciallady Awareness team, helping to donate sanitary products to schools and medical supplies to hospitals. It was a joy to be a part of another successful initiative aimed at supporting women's health and combating menstrual poverty, which was the theme of the book launch decided to participate in.

The book launch preparation was an eye-opener for me as it made me realise who was truly there for me in times of need. I was fortunate enough to have the support of amazing individuals such as Honourable John Boadu, who went above and beyond to help me.

A few days before the book launch, I had the opportunity to be interviewed on United Television Ghana Limited (UTV) and Peace FM, two of the prominent TV broadcasters in Ghana. The interview was well-detailed and allowed me to explain why I decided to share my story with the world.

During the interview, I also talked about my upcoming book launch and expressed my gratitude to all the sponsors and partners involved in the event. When I am interviewed, I make sure that I provide adequate information and answers to every question asked.

After I left the station, articles about my story were published and my book was promoted on their social networking website. I was grateful to Kennedy Osei Esq, CEO of United Television Ghana Limited, for his generosity. Although he could not attend my book launch, I sent him an invitation and he gave me the opportunity to be interviewed. He also instructed his staff to promote my book and use their platform to help more people learn about my story and my advocacy work. After publishing my story, I received an overwhelming response from readers who not only read my story but also started following me on social media platforms like Instagram and Facebook. Some even sent me messages to express their support and encouragement, describing me as brave and urging me to continue my good work.

As I reflected on the events leading up to the book launch, a particular incident came to mind. When I arrived in Accra just two days prior to the book launch, I felt exhausted and overwhelmed with stress as I prayed for the success of the launch preparations.

One evening, while travelling back to the lakeside estate where I was staying. I fell asleep in the back of the cab. Suddenly, I woke up to the sound of Miriam screaming and the driver struggling to stop the car. Despite his efforts, the car continued moving and the driver repeatedly stated that his brakes were not working.

In that moment of panic, I screamed 'JESUS' twice and to my relief, the car came to an emergency stop. It was a terrifying experience, but I was grateful that we were all safe.

Within seconds, a big truck appeared out of nowhere without any lights or hazard lights on and crossed in front of us. I screamed, "Jesus, thank you!" because our cab was able to brake in time. I am sure we would have collided with the truck and potentially suffered serious injury or even death. The speed at which the truck was travelling was so great that I did not think any of us would have survived the impact.

This experience left me extremely frightened and I could not stop thinking about the potential collision with the truck. The thought of never being able to experience life again or being seriously injured haunted me for days. It made me wonder if it was a sign that I was rushing too much and whether I should reconsider the book launch.

I was experiencing uncertainty about the success and value of my book launch, and I began to question if the effort I put into it was worthwhile. Despite having doubts and concerns, I acknowledged that significant success requires effort and the ability to tune out distractions and fears.

As I contemplated whether to continue or quit the book launch, I realised the importance of taking a step back and reflecting on my goals and motivations for writing the book. I asked myself what inspired me to write it, what I hoped to achieve and if I had met those goals. Additionally, I questioned my reason for launching the book in the first place. Was it only to raise funds to support women's healthcare and combat menstrual poverty or did I want to share a deeper purpose and message with the world?

It's natural to experience doubts and concerns following a significant project such as a book launch. However, success is not always immediate and it can take time for a book to gain recognition and traction. Instead of focusing solely on the outcome, it is important to also consider the process and the reasons behind your decision to write and launch the book.

Reflecting on my goals and motivations has helped provide clarity and perspective on the value and impact of my book launch. I knew that my reason for writing the book was to make a positive impact on the world and encourage other women and young girls suffering from gynaecological conditions to seek early medical intervention.

Furthermore, based on the feedback and response, I have received from readers and reviewers, I was pleased to report that readers have responded positively to my work. However, I did encounter significant challenges in getting support for the preparation of the book launch. Despite the positive reception, the level of support for this project has been quite limited.

After reflecting on the success of my book, I realised that even though it had not yielded much monetary gain, it had been widely received by major academic platforms and archives. Moreover, its availability for purchase in most countries was a significant accomplishment in its own right. Instead of being discouraged by the trials that had occurred, I understood that they were simply forms of temporary setbacks. As a result, I resolved to remain focused on striving for even greater achievements.

I then decided to focus on working even harder to achieve outstanding results. Despite facing several challenges, I persevered with the support of my friends, which was a crucial factor in the success of the book launch.

However, just three days before the launch, another incident occurred. I was travelling from Madina to Lakeside in a cab after collecting leaflets and other items for the launch. During the rush hour, the cab suddenly stopped in the middle of a busy road without warning, causing a large truck to come to a sudden halt as well.

The unexpected incident resulted in a massive traffic jam and a crowd started to gather, which made me feel anxious and scared.

Other road users quickly rushed to the cab as the driver got out upon their insistence to check his car tyres. The tyre had burst severely and the bystanders kept expressing how fortunate I was that God was watching over me.

I was shaking and at a loss for words. My mind went blank and I did not understand what was happening. One of the men who had approached the cab asked if he could give me a lift or find me another cab. He asked so many questions, but my brain was in a fog and I could not give him a proper answer. I sat down in a nearby seating area while other road users tried to fix the cab's car tyre.

After sitting for a few minutes, I called a friend to come pick me up, but as soon as I hung up, I called back and said I would take another cab home, so I didn't need the lift.

My body and mind underwent a series of physiological and psychological responses which had a significant impact on me. I was still traumatised.

The shock was a sudden and unexpected event or experience that I believe was very traumatic, distressing and emotionally overwhelming.

I could feel a rapid heart rate, increased blood pressure, shallow breathing and sweating. My body was responding to the perceived danger of what had happened.

I knew I had to come out of the sudden shock before it transmitted to a more serious shock and possibly resulted in prolonged side effects.

However, I understood that a prolonged response to the event could have negative effects on the body and possibly develop chronic stress.

I felt a range of emotions such as fear, anxiety, confusion, anger and sadness.

As I checked in at Kotoka International Airport for my flight to Kumasi, I murmured to myself that I was looking forward to a good rest and relaxing time.

I took a very early flight.

I arrived in Kumasi at 7 a.m. and took a cab home from the airport. During the ride, I enjoyed the sights of the city and its diverse neighbourhoods and suburbs. Along the way, I spotted many grocery stores that prompted me to buy some items.

When I arrived at my aunt's house, I was warmly welcomed and treated to a delicious breakfast.

After finishing my meal, I immediately retired to bed and dozed off for roughly three hours. Upon waking up, I found that lunch was already prepared and I indulged in another delicious meal before feeling fatigued again and returning to bed. It dawned on me that I had been spending most of my time eating and sleeping. As I reflected on my experience in Accra, I began to understand how stressful life in the city could be.

After a couple of days, I had grown tired of the monotonous routine of eating, sleeping and lazing about.

I realised that lazing about had several disadvantages. I became unproductive and did not feel useful as all I did throughout the day was eat and sleep. This lifestyle could have a negative impact on my health, especially since I had already experienced fear and panic as a result of two near-accidents. Spending all day eating and lying in bed left me feeling endlessly tired.

I began to recognise that time is a valuable resource and when a person is lazing about, they are wasting their time. This can lead to missed opportunities, regrets and an overall feeling of dissatisfaction.

I began to realise that my laziness was having a negative impact on my relationships with others. I was not communicating with my friends and acquaintances as much as I used to, and I wasn't putting in any effort. I spent most of my time sleeping. As time went on, I came to the realisation that I needed to change. As a result, I decided to leave my aunt's house and move to a hotel with Miriam who joined me from Accra.

I was invited to speak at the Rotary Club of Kumasi about the aftermath of my book launch. The meeting took place at Lancaster Kumasi City, a beautiful hotel with modern decor.

Upon arriving, I was introduced by the speaker of the meeting to the seated members. As I took my seat at the Rotary Club of Kumasi, I immediately felt welcomed by the warm and inviting atmosphere. I began to share the story behind my book, explaining what inspired me to write it. In addition, I expressed my gratitude for the club's collaboration with my NGO and their valuable contribution to our fundraising efforts. The members of the Rotary Club were receptive and supportive, offering suggestions for future collaborations and potential projects. Their praise and appreciation for my efforts were truly humbling and uplifting.

The meeting lasted an hour and afterwards, we mingled and networked.

After the meeting, Nana Effah, Prince Prempeh, Miriam and I decided to go out for dinner. We had a wonderful time and the evening was truly fabulous.

Chapter 8
Life Is Worth Living

While I was in Kumasi, Ghana, I had the incredible opportunity to be interviewed by Zionfelix, a renowned Ghanaian blogger, YouTuber and social media marketer. I was absolutely amazed when he requested to interview me, considering his impressive online presence with over 2.3 million Instagram followers, more than 550,000 YouTube subscribers and a staggering 400,000 followers on Facebook. Zionfelix is undeniably Ghana's most followed blogger and I could not contain my excitement at the prospect of gaining significant exposure in Ghana through this interview.

The mere thought of the interview filled me with thrill and anticipation, knowing that it would undoubtedly enhance my visibility and reach. With Zionfelix's substantial subscriber base and loyal following, I was confident that the interview would enable me to connect with a broader audience. By seizing the opportunity to engage in a conversation with Zionfelix, I was poised to share my story with a vast array of viewers and tap into their dedicated community.

On the interview day, I was excited to share my story. He was also relaxed and made the interview go effortlessly.

I knew this was going to have a significant increase in the visibility of your book and my NGO.

Also, being interviewed was going to enhance my credibility and reputation. Zionfelix endorsement or association could lend legitimacy to my interview and help me establish myself as a trusted personality in the advocacy work.

When I returned to Accra, I had only a few days left before heading back to the UK. During that time, I diligently attended numerous meetings. It was important for me to fulfil all my scheduled meeting commitments and ensure productive outcomes.

When I arrived in the UK, I reflected on my whole trip to Ghana and all the incidents that happened prior to me visiting Ghana and upon my return. Indeed it was a deep emotional thinking. But the experience made me understand not to expect people to do good things for you, since some may possibly let you down and this can really hurt and affect your self-esteem and confidence. Also, I realised time, especially hard time plays a significant role in revealing a person's true personality. Because, the people I was interacting with or relating to did not reveal their characteristics from the beginning, but after an extended period. I become aware of their attidodem opportunity to observe their behaviour, actions and responses to various situations. This prolonged exposure allowed me to gather a more accurate understanding of their true selves.

It is true that patterns in behaviour become more evident as time progresses. I began to notice recurring tendencies, reactions and choices that reflect the other person's values, beliefs and motivations. These patterns offer valuable insights into their character and provide a deeper understanding of who they are as individuals.

Moreover, as time passes, people tend to drop their initial facades and reveal their authentic selves. This is seen at the beginning of the early stages of a relationship or acquaintance; individuals may consciously or unconsciously present a polished or idealised version of themselves.

However, as familiarity grows, they may become more comfortable and relaxed, allowing their true nature to shine through.

Hence, exercising patience and remaining observant are essential when building relationships or getting to know someone. I perceived that rushing to conclusions based on first impressions could be misleading. Thus, I allowed time to unfold, this gave me the opportunity to assess the person's consistency, integrity and authenticity more accurately.

During the process of getting to know my friends or people I thought genuinely cared about me time granted me the opportunity to witness how people handle challenges, conflicts and various life situations. By observing their responses and actions during difficult times, I gained valuable insights into their resilience, problem-solving skills, empathy and overall character.

I understand that time is a powerful tool for uncovering a person's true personality. But through patient observation and prolonged interaction, I knew I could discern patterns in behaviour understand values and motivations, and gain a more accurate understanding of the people I thought were my friends. It went through this process and I realised, I foster genuine connections and build meaningful relationships based on a deeper appreciation of each other's true selves.

2022 was a year of reflection. Everything I went through served as motivation, despite the sudden and challenging pain that persisted throughout the year.

As I reflected on what transpired, I noticed significant growth in my mental and emotional well-being. Additionally, I started to question why I had not severed ties with them earlier and allowed this situation to persist for such an extended period of time.

Although I have questioned life's challenges and faced setbacks caused by dishonest people, what I failed to notice is that these experiences have actually helped me build confidence.

The confidence I built helped me in my personal development and growth. I have learnt to believe in myself and my abilities; I am more likely to take on new challenges, set ambitious goals and strive for success. The experience helped me overcome self-doubt and fear which enabled me to step out of my comfort zone and explore new opportunities without fear.

I have built a resilience spirit, therefore, when faced with setbacks and failures, the experience has provided me with the strength and determination to bounce back from difficult situations. I believe that the challenges I have faced have helped me view failures as valuable learning experiences and have enabled me to persevere in the face of adversity. The confidence I have developed has greatly contributed to fostering a positive self-image. As a result, I now genuinely feel good about myself and my abilities and this positivity emanates through my actions, behaviour and interactions with others.

I vividly remember the times when I used to worry about being let down by people. However, I have noticed a significant shift in how others perceive me. They now regard me as more competent and trustworthy, which has consequently led to the cultivation of stronger social and professional relationships.

The setbacks I have encountered have had a profoundly positive impact on various aspects of my life. I have witnessed significant improvements in my research abilities, financial stability and emotional well-being. Moreover, my communication skills have undergone a remarkable transformation. I can confidently assert that I am now more self-assured, willing to take calculated risks, make informed decisions and perform at my utmost potential.

One of my most remarkable achievements has been overcoming my fears and anxieties, which were substantial obstacles that hindered my ability to seek help and open up about my struggles. Through bolstered confidence and improved self-esteem, I have effectively combated these negative emotions. Particularly, acknowledging and accepting my diagnosis has empowered me to utilise my experiences as a purposeful means of assisting others.

This journey has provided me with the opportunity to confront my fears directly, challenge limiting beliefs and take the necessary steps to overcome them. It has empowered me to approach situations with a positive mindset, thereby reducing anxiety levels and fostering personal growth.

Embarking on this transformative journey has made me more assertive. I can confidently state that my increased self-confidence and improved self-esteem have given me the ability to express my thoughts, ideas and opinions with clarity.

It has enabled me to stand up for myself when I feel my rights have been infringed upon and has also provided me with the strength to set boundaries and communicate effectively in both personal and professional settings.

If I did not go through trials in life, I am sure I would not have the confidence or be able to set higher goals, work diligently towards them and persevere until I achieve them. Surely, the outcome of the traumatised situations has given me the confidence that I am capable of achieving greatness, which fuels my motivation and determination to succeed.

Experiencing life challenges is crucial for personal growth, resilience, positive self-image, improved performance, overcoming fear and anxiety, assertiveness and achieving success. It has empowered me to embrace opportunities, overcome obstacles and lead a fulfilling and successful life.

Self-care has become incredibly important to me. Reflecting on my past experiences and traumas, I realised that I had neglected my own well-being, happiness and overall perspective on life. It is truly remarkable to witness how my purpose has evolved into being a voice for other women and young girls.

However, I have also come to realise that I had not established clear boundaries between personal exhaustion and making a positive impact on others' lives. When I initially shared my story and founded Speciallady Awareness, it was uplifting and I always felt a sense of duty to listen and dedicate a significant amount of time to supporting women and young girls who were suffering from gynaecological conditions or simply seeking mentorship or general support.

There were some days when I found myself in the hospital or experiencing a flare-up of my condition. Despite my circumstances, whenever a message or phone call came through regarding Speciallady Awareness initiatives or mentoring someone, I felt compelled to answer and address the issue at hand. Even when my husband kindly advised me to take some time for myself and prioritise self-care, my initial reaction was defensive. I believed that if I did not attend to every request or incident, it meant I had not fulfilled my calling. I must admit that on certain days, this overwhelming pressure becomes too much to handle.

When I partake in my therapy sessions, I learn that in as much as I have compassion, I must learn to give myself the tenderness and care I need when I am going through a tough time or experiencing flare-ups.

It was indeed I had not exercised self-compassion hence, I was not feeling fulfilled most times.

Indeed, it is easier to say, "I will take care of my feelings, myself and prioritise my mental health," but putting those practices into action has been challenging for me. I have been struggling to find a balance between compassion for others and practising self-compassion. I have noticed the negative effects of neglecting my self-care. While my insomnia has improved over the last few months compared to previous years, there are still days when I find it difficult to sleep or establish a healthy sleep routine.

I have made the decision to prioritise my self-care and have implemented several measures to achieve this. To begin with, I have established clear boundaries within my NGO, Speciallady Awareness initiatives. I have taken steps to recruit qualified and experienced volunteers who can carry out outreach projects in schools and communities, even in my absence from Ghana. By empowering the team coordinators to generate ideas, and suggestions and organise the programs, I have allowed them to take the lead and showcase their leadership qualities. This transition took place in December 2022 and I am delighted and proud to have a capable team that can successfully execute similar projects with or without my physical presence in Ghana.

When Speciallady Awareness partnered with the National Academy of Student Achievements Awards Ghana to conduct outreach activities at the Ghana Communication Technology University, Ghana Institute of Journalism, Valley View University and University of Winneba, the volunteers visited these educational institutions on behalf of the organisation. Instead of personally flying out to Ghana, I provided assistance by conducting research on the topics that were to be presented to the students.

I played a role in preparing potential questions and answers, as well as crafting a narrative explaining the establishment of Speciallady Awareness. By collaborating with the volunteers remotely, I contributed to the overall preparations for the outreach activities and ensured that the necessary information was available for engaging and informative presentations to the students.

I was fascinated to witness the team's impressive expertise and their ability to deliver presentations with confidence and passion. Although a part of me was concerned about potential challenges, such as the team panicking in my absence or facing difficult questions they could not answer, I realised that these were circumstances beyond my control.

Instead of worrying about them, I chose to maintain a positive mindset and hope for the best.

Speciallady Awareness mission success is crucial, in order to achieve this recruiting the right team such as volunteers play a vital role in carrying out the mission and goals of a charity. They surely contribute their time, skills and energy to support an organisation's activities and initiatives. The volunteers could extend the NGO's reach and capacity to make a positive impact on its cause.

The volunteers I recruited from December 2022, increased the manpower and resources.

For many years, Speciallady Awareness has operated with limited staff and resources. Hence, the volunteers have provided additional manpower and skills which has helped expand the NGO's capabilities. Visiting four universities within four weeks was a massive success and I was so grateful to Annah Okrah for leading the team.

The support of volunteers has helped accomplish more than it could with its core staff alone.

Amazing volunteers like Sylvia, Miriam, Naa Kwaley, Papa Yaw, Samuel have brought a wide range of backgrounds, experiences, and expertise to the table. They possess valuable skills in areas such as marketing, communications, negotiation and project management.

Their diverse perspectives and knowledge have tapped into a broader pool of ideas, creativity and problem-solving abilities.

They have been involved in various community projects prior to volunteering for Speciallady Awareness.

Sylvia Davis, the lead coordinator mostly acts as an ambassador, spreads awareness about the charity's work, engages with the community and has been building relationships with potential donors, sponsors and partners.

Having dedicated and hardworking volunteers has been invaluable in saving the Speciallady Awareness funds, especially during the challenging times brought on by the Covid-19 pandemic. The organisation has faced funding struggles, but thanks to the commitment of our volunteers, we have managed to overcome many obstacles.

Moreover, the involvement of volunteers has enabled us to reduce expenses associated with hiring additional staff. This cost-saving measure has allowed Speciallady Awareness to allocate its resources more effectively, channelling funds towards program development and other essential areas.

Given the current financial crisis, Speciallady Awareness has been operating within limited budgets. By actively recruiting volunteers, we can mitigate some of the financial challenges we face, ensuring smoother operations and financial stability for the organisation.

I have always ensured that all Speciallady Awareness volunteers have development and personal growth.

I strongly believe volunteering should offer individuals an opportunity to contribute to a cause they care about, develop new skills and gain valuable experience. By providing meaningful volunteer opportunities, it can attract motivated individuals who are eager to learn, grow and make a difference. This can lead to long-term relationships with volunteers who may become supporters, advocates or found their own charitable organisations.

Witnessing that I have managed to get volunteers to assist Speciallady Awareness initiatives, it has become very clear that this has reduced some of the stress I was going through.

I have also recognised the importance of setting boundaries in the way I conduct my mentoring sessions and respond to messages and requests. As a result, I have made the decision to ask people who seek advice from me to schedule a meeting instead of providing the service immediately.

Implementing this approach will help alleviate any pressure I may feel and contribute positively to my mental health and overall well-being. Although it was challenging for me to make these decisions, I understand that self-care is not something that can be easily practised.

I have assessed the importance of prioritising my overall health, particularly my mental well-being. Consequently, I have chosen to focus on what holds the utmost significance in order to gather the strength necessary to pursue my purpose.

The persistent occurrence of chronic pains and infections has significantly affected me. Therefore, it is imperative for me to acknowledge that placing my health and well-being at the forefront is of utmost importance.

Some of the people who contacted me understood my request and booked appointments others, did not contact me again.

Although I felt like I let them down, I had to remind myself of my health and well-being.

Furthermore, this experience provided me with an opportunity to promote my debut book, which recounts my journey of pursuing medical intervention despite facing trauma, disappointments and neglect. Those who have read the book have expressed how it has inspired and encouraged them to proactively seek medical advice when they notice signs related to their health. I have personally observed that as I took this step, I felt less exhausted and had more quality time to spend with my family while prioritising my own well-being.

When I arrived from Ghana at the end of November 2023, I began experiencing body pains, fatigue and anxiety. I attributed these symptoms to the exhaustion and stress of organising the book launch. I took painkillers and attempted to avoid excessive worry. However, the pains persisted sporadically and were accompanied by occasional fever.

During Christmas 2022, I experienced similar episodes, but I chose to overlook the symptoms and focus on spending quality time with my family, including my sister and her family.

I ruled out stress as the reason for not being able to find suitable work that accommodates my health. I recently moved to Chilwell (Nottinghamshire) as part of my husband's army assignment postings, and it may take a couple of months for me to settle into a job. However, I am eager to start working to avoid getting bored staying at home. Moreover, there's nothing quite like the joy of having a steady income to achieve financial independence.

Self-care has remained a top priority for me, particularly due to the persistent occurrence of chronic pains. Despite that, I managed to secure a part-time job, which involved a six-week training period where I had to sit for extended hours before getting a break. After attending the initial two days of training, I began experiencing hot flashes and lower back pains. Despite staying hydrated by drinking plenty of water, I noticed my urine had a yellowish colour and I started feeling nauseous and fatigued. Regrettably, the pain persisted, and I ultimately had to make the difficult decision to quit the job.

After explaining the unfortunate circumstances to my GP over a phone call, she requested that I visit her at the doctor's surgery the following day. As I arrived at the genuine doctor's surgery, I could not help but reflect on the amount of time I have spent attending doctor's appointments and medical consultations.

On the day when I live a pain-free lifestyle and no longer have to attend hospital consultations, I will be utterly captivated by the beauty of that moment.

I guess all of these were mere dreams, wishes I can only hope for. My name was called and I obediently followed the receptionist's instructions as I made my way towards the consultation rooms of the doctors.

As I entered, a warm smile greeted me from the doctor, who gestured towards a chair and asked me to have a seat. The sharp pain I was experiencing made it difficult for me to sit, but after a moment's struggle, I managed to lower myself into the chair and returned the smile, albeit weakly. The doctor noticed the anguish on my face and inquired about my well-being, as the pain seemed evident. I explained to her the immense difficulty I was facing in finding a comfortable position, whether it was sitting, standing, or even lying down.

She asked whether I needed stronger painkillers since it was evident that the ones I had been taking were not sufficient. I explained to her my urgent need to see a specialist as I was increasingly concerned about the sudden pains. In fact, I had to quit my job because I realised I could not sit for extended periods and one of the job requirements was precisely that.

Feeling disheartened, I asked her if there was anything that could be done promptly to alleviate the pain.

Unfortunately, the more I yearned for a solution, the more it seemed unattainable. Thankfully, she empathised with my situation and granted me a medical leave of at least three months. She also advised me to prioritise getting adequate rest while she reached out to the hospital to expedite the process of finding a specialist for me as soon as possible.

As I returned home, tears streamed down my face as I drove. The pain and disappointment engulfed me, shattering my heart. All I yearned for was strength and fulfilment through meaningful work. It's disheartening to realise that my dream career remains elusive, but I understand that it's not the most pressing concern at the moment.

Whispering to myself, I reassured myself that this was just a phase and it would pass with time. However, as I continued to stay home, each passing day brought more stress, boredom and dissatisfaction with life. I longed to be productive, to have a steady income and to make financial contributions to the household.

A stable financial breakthrough became my ultimate aspiration.

However, the intensity of the pain continued to escalate, reaching unbearable levels. It severely impacted my ability to sleep, leading to a resurgence of insomnia. Despite my relentless efforts to find relief, none of the remedies I tried provided any success. Frustrated and desperate, I found myself making weekly calls to the doctor's surgery, anxiously inquiring about when the obstetrics and gynaecology department would finally reach out to investigate the underlying cause of my excruciating pain. However, each time I contacted the doctor, they would simply reassure me that the hospital would get in touch with me at the appropriate time.

I asked God why He was allowing me to go through such challenging situations, feeling upset and questioning why I had to continue suffering despite the traumas, disappointments and setbacks I had endured. Life felt incredibly unfair and cruel.

In my plea, I questioned when God would grant me the ability to enjoy life without constantly worrying about my future health. And then, a few days later, a glimmer of hope emerged. The doctors called to inform me that they had found a consultant at one of the reputable hospitals in Nottingham and I would soon receive an appointment letter.

This news brought a sense of reassurance, as I believed that the help I needed and some much-needed explanations for my pain and triggers were finally within reach. I felt an overwhelming sense of happiness and eagerly looked forward to the upcoming appointment.

I was waiting impatiently for the specialist to send an appointment letter through.

A few days had passed when the doctor called me once again, delivering the long-awaited news. They had successfully located an expert who possesses extensive experience in dealing with my unique anatomy. Furthermore, this specialist would be collaborating closely with an endometriosis expert. The overwhelming sense of relief brought tears to my eyes, knowing that they had finally found a gynaecologist who specialises in uterus didelphys with severe endometriosis.

I was a living testament to the doctor's exceptional attentiveness during our previous meeting. I had emphasised my strong desire to receive care from a gynaecologist who had treated women with similar wombs as mine. It was a wish fulfilled and I could not have been more grateful for the dedication and understanding they displayed.

There have been moments when I deeply reflect on my life, my health and the path I decided to embark on as 'Special Lady'—being the voice for those suffering in silence from gynaecological conditions. When I experience pain and am unable to work due to a flare-up, it compels me to delve into profound contemplation.

Furthermore, I deeply appreciate the goodness of God. Firstly, for guiding me this far and being by my side throughout countless hospital appointments, surgeries, miscarriages and premature childbirth. Additionally, I am grateful for the opportunity to write the book and all the wonderful experiences that have unfolded in my life.

The more I contemplated my health and life, the greater my realisation of the significance of self-care. It was high time for me to prioritise self-care in my life and I believe that by doing so, I will experience greater satisfaction and kindness towards myself.

I realised that the constant rumination and questioning had run its course and it was time for me to put an end to it. Instead, I made a conscious choice to shift my focus towards maintaining a positive attitude. By acknowledging my potential, I was confident that numerous opportunities would present themselves.

I realised that knowing my potential in life was of paramount importance as it would empower me to unlock my true capabilities, pursue my passions and achieve meaningful success.

Also, understanding my potential will help me recognise my unique talents, skills, strengths and personal qualities that can be harnessed to accomplish my goals and make a positive impact on the world around me. This has been transformative in some aspects of my life.

The trauma and pain I have experienced gave me the ability to set realistic and achievable goals. I have gained a clear understanding of my strengths and abilities; I can set targets that align with my capabilities, enabling me to make steady progress towards my aspirations. This self-awareness has allowed me to focus my time, energy and resources on areas where I have the greatest potential for success, increasing the likelihood of achieving my objectives.

Hence, being the voice and sharing my story on a global scale have given me a sense of pride and fulfilment.

Furthermore, recognising my potential has enabled me to make informed decisions about my life choices and personal development. I believe that by understanding my natural inclinations and aptitudes, I can make choices that align with my strengths and passions.

This will be useful in enhancing my job satisfaction and increase my chances of excelling in my advocacy work.

I have noticed that by engaging in activities that capitalise on my abilities, I have experienced a sense of fulfilment, enthusiasm and purpose in my endeavours.

Discovering my potential has instilled confidence and self-belief.

I can now say, I have a clear understanding of what I am capable of therefore, I can approach challenges with a positive mindset. Being aware of my abilities helps me overcome self-doubt and fear of failure.

I have recognised that I have what it takes to overcome obstacles and achieve success. This self-assurance encourages me to take calculated risks, explore new opportunities and continuously strive for personal growth.

Notwithstanding, I have an understanding of my potential, which allows me to leverage my strengths in collaborative endeavours. I believe that since I became aware of my contributions, I can seek out partnerships and collaborations that complement my abilities.

By working with individuals who possess different strengths and skill sets, I know now I can create synergistic relationships that lead to innovative solutions and collective achievements.

Since recognising my potential, I have been able to develop an inclusive environment, promoting teamwork and mutual growth.

I have gained a strong sense of fulfilment such as embracing a growth mindset and being open to learning and development.

This has allowed me to continuously tap into new potentials and push the boundaries of what I thought was possible.

Throughout my journey, I have discovered and cultivated new talents acquired valuable skills and actively pursued opportunities for personal and professional growth. By doing so, I have unlocked even greater potential within myself. A prime illustration of this transformation occurred during my pursuit of a master's degree program. Initially, I lacked confidence when it came to delivering presentations in front of a small audience. The challenges of presentations and public speaking used to evoke fear within me, regardless of how well-prepared I was. Surprisingly, my confidence has flourished significantly ever since I made the brave decision to publicly share my story and became a woman reproductive health advocate.

And I am delighted knowing my potential has given me personal fulfilment, goal achievement and overall success in becoming an inspiration to other women and young girls suffering from gynaecological conditions.

The journey has empowered me to make informed decisions, set realistic goals, build confidence and leverage my strengths.

I have understood and developed my potential, which has led to a purposeful and meaningful life while making a positive impact on the world around me.

When I made the decision to embark on writing a second book, my mind became inundated with numerous questions. I found myself pondering whether people would be inclined to read it and what factors would serve as their motivation.

I also contemplated whether my book could inspire and provide guidance to individuals grappling with life's obstacles. Why did I believe that my life experiences could offer them encouragement and serve as a source of guidance?

Although these questions plagued my mind, I also believed that my second book could serve as an inspiration for many.

Not only does it provide motivation during challenging circumstances, but it also offers guidance for introspection and fulfilling our purpose on this earth.

I had the incredible opportunity to be featured in My Story Magazine (MSM), an entrepreneurial digital media platform that showcases the life journeys of entrepreneurs from Ghana and beyond.

MSM has gained recognition for its coverage of prominent and influential personalities in Ghana. It is truly an honour to have been a part of such a prestigious publication. When the magazine edition was released, I was overwhelmed with joy.

Chapter 9
Hope in the Season of Dismay

It can be overwhelming and distressing when trying to navigate your inner emotions and the challenges of life. Here we are, in the year 2023, seven years after the discovery of my rare congenital abnormality and the subsequent diagnoses of my other reproductive health disorders. I had hoped that by now, the pains, recurrent infections and complications would have subsided or at least lessened. Unfortunately, it seems that the joy I experience from witnessing any sudden improvements can only be short-lived.

The constant worry and uncertainty about the future persist, refusing to leave me alone. There have been countless moments where I have questioned whether I am trapped in a dream or if this is my reality. At times, I find myself isolating from others, which occasionally concerns my husband.

When family gatherings are approaching, I often find myself making excuses to avoid attending. On some occasions, he tries to empathise and respects my decision not to go, but there are times when he insists and ends up arguing about the importance of making an effort.

Personally, I sometimes struggle to comprehend the necessity of getting closer to people. It is not that I have anything against them, but I simply value my peace and prioritise my health.

Especially, when the lower back and waist pains worsen, I cannot sit for more than thirty minutes without experiencing discomfort. This becomes particularly challenging during family gatherings, where I find it difficult to stand up without experiencing pain. Just imagine this happening during one of those episodes; the questions, the curious glances and the comments, whether well-intentioned or merely out of curiosity, can really affect me emotionally.

On the occasions when I have managed to attend these gatherings, I have fervently prayed to God to avoid such episodes. So I go there and try to act as if nothing is happening, appearing well-dressed, maintaining a cheerful demeanour and making an effort to engage with everyone.

One might attribute it to age and the changes that come with life, but deep within my heart, I know that I am the kind of person who thrives in the company of others. I am the type who revels in engaging activities, enjoys spending time with loved ones and cherishes the bonds of family and friendship.

However, my life has undergone significant transformations and while there have been positive developments; there are also moments when I long for deeper connections. I yearn for the ability to be honest about my feelings regarding my life, health and overall well-being.

In our world, it often seems that people fixate on superficial appearances, the expectations they impose on others and how they use pain and struggles as tools for judging one another.

Hence, these are the reasons why I have decided to make some changes. I cannot bear the thought of being a burden to those who truly love me. It becomes increasingly difficult for me to constantly express my fear of life's uncertainties, especially considering my medical conditions such as bowel endometriosis, adhesions, multiple fibroids and my unique anatomy (uterus didelphys). These factors make me highly susceptible to various gynaecological complications, including cancer and kidney diseases.

Even when I receive invitations to events, conferences, or simple occasions like weddings, getaways, or birthdays, I find myself caught in similar thoughts. I worry that I might attend and enjoy the gathering for a short while, only to be plagued by thoughts of how others will feel if I suddenly experience intense pain or discomfort.

I vividly recall the moment when I received my diagnosis of bowel endometriosis, along with adhesions and other related conditions. The surgeon shared some insights and emphasised that my life was about to undergo a significant transformation. Although certain treatments could provide temporary relief, the symptoms would inevitably resurface over time, necessitating multiple surgeries.

The surgeon reassured me that this pattern was common among women dealing with four-stage endometriosis.

Having four-stage endometriosis is already challenging, but being a woman with uterus didelphys, which entails having two wombs, two cervixes and two vaginal canals, exacerbates the severity of my endometriosis. The presence of this condition can give rise to a range of complications, including repeated pregnancy loss, kidney issues, low birth weight and various pregnancy-related complications such as miscarriage, stillbirth, or premature childbirth. Additionally, individuals with uterus didelphys are more prone to developing gynaecological conditions.

Having thoroughly researched the illness, it all made sense why I keep experiencing the symptoms. According to scientific research, endometriosis stage 4 can cause chronic and unrelenting pelvic pain, as well as severe menstrual cramps that often require time off from work and social engagements. Moreover, it can make sexual intercourse painful, which can have a negative impact on intimacy and relationships. The burden of these symptoms can lead to feelings of depression, anxiety, and isolation.

Stage IV endometriosis is recognised as the most severe form of endometriosis. It is characterised by the presence of extensive deep and superficial growths resembling endometrial tissue within the reproductive tract. Additionally, it can affect other organs in the pelvic region and abdomen. Infertility is strongly associated with stage IV endometriosis.

Thick adhesions develop throughout the pelvic region, resulting in the formation of widespread scar tissue. While most medical professionals I have spoken to during my hospital consultations state that stage IV endometriosis is not typically considered a fatal disease, they do acknowledge that it can give rise to dangerous and potentially life-threatening complications, significantly impacting one's quality of life.

The constant worry and uncertainty surrounding my health always make me very sad. Crying sometimes and forcing myself to ignore the whole situation sometimes have a toll on me.

It is easier not to share my worry with people.

And even though I have shared my story globally about discovering my rare congenital abnormality and the medical complications I face; I still encounter people who make unnecessary comments or suggestions regarding my health. This is particularly evident when it comes to discussions about childbearing. Despite my openness about my situation, many individuals continue to question when I am planning to have a second child and why I am leaving it until late, considering my daughter is nearly a teenager.

It is quite shocking how people feel entitled to have opinions about others' lives. Perhaps this stems from society's tendency to impose timelines or expectations on individuals. This becomes particularly problematic when it comes to individuals facing medical conditions that impact their ability to conceive or carry a child to full term.

Unfortunately, many people lack an understanding of the various types of infertility. It's important to recognise that someone may struggle to have more than one child and we should not impose our beliefs on them or expect them to conform to our own choices and actions.

Some women may never be able to conceive or give birth due to health complications or personal choice and it is completely acceptable and valid. Regardless of the reasons, it is important for society to show respect and understanding towards such decisions or choices.

In my own situation, as a woman suffering from stage endometriosis and uterine didelphys, my chances of conceiving are extremely slim or carrying a foetus to full term presents even greater challenges. These conditions significantly complicate matters for me, making the journey even more difficult.

But, I also believe in miracles and God's interventions. There have been many situations in my life that I must confess God has been good to me and delivered me.

It seems I have to continue to explain myself or my conditions whenever I am questioned as to why I only have one child and when am I going to have another one.

I have grown mentally strong not to take people's comments negatively or use the opportunity to educate them on reproductive health disorders.

Sometimes, I turn those types of comments to raise awareness while other times, I just ignore the comments.

However, I also firmly believe in miracles and divine interventions. There have been numerous instances in my life where I must admit that God has been exceedingly kind to me and provided deliverance.

It seems that I am constantly compelled to justify or clarify my circumstances whenever I am questioned about why I have only one child and when I plan to have another. Over time, I have developed mental resilience to avoid taking such comments in a negative light and I often seize the opportunity to educate people about reproductive health disorders.

Occasionally, I transform these types of comments into opportunities to raise awareness, while at other times; I simply choose to disregard them altogether.

There is a saying that highlights the significance of our reactions to life events. While we may not always have control over what happens to us, we do have control over how we respond to those events. Our reactions, attitudes and choices play a crucial role in shaping our experiences and determining the outcomes we achieve.

I have learnt that when I am faced with unexpected circumstances or challenges, the way I choose to react can make a significant difference in our lives. I need to maintain a positive mindset, seeking solutions or answers and adapting to change.

By taking these measures, I can navigate difficult situations more effectively. Hence the way I respond to life events can impact our emotional well-being, relationships and overall outlook on life.

I always need to understand that my reactions are not always easy to control, as I can be influenced by various factors such as my personality, past experiences and current challenging circumstances. Regardless of all these complications I need to develop skills and strategies to better manage my responses to such life trials. Acknowledging the significance of the challenging times, having self-reflection and emotional intelligence can help me cultivate a greater sense of awareness and control over my reactions.

Moreover, my reactions can also influence the way others perceive me and interact with me. A calm and composed response in the face of adversity can inspire confidence in those around me and foster a supportive environment. This seems to be the hardest part at times. Whenever I face adversities, I tend to become angry with life and question why I have to go through such trauma repeatedly. However, allowing these negative reactions to take over only creates unnecessary tension and hinders productive problem-solving in some cases.

It is normal to feel the weight of such challenging times, but I am still learning to understand that how I react to these setbacks is more important than how I perceive them. I am fully aware that I cannot control every aspect of my life, but recognising that my reactions hold significant power will help me grow mentally and emotionally, ultimately impacting my well-being and health in a significant way.

By acknowledging this, I can actively work towards personal growth and resilience.

The journey has empowered me to work on myself, from having effective communication to understanding others' perspectives in life and achievements.

It has helped me in my life choices and the circle I have now.

Although, the journey has made me wary of people and their true intentions.

The more I get exposed to people; I learn not to judge a book by its cover and also to note that not all that glitter is gold.

Many individuals may present themselves as highly positive and influential figures on social networks. However, it is crucial to exercise caution in determining who we consider as role models or mentors, especially once we have the opportunity to know them on a personal level.

I get thrilled when I have the opportunity to meet people whom I initially perceived as role models, only to discover that they are continuously focused on their own personal growth.

There have been several occasions when I have developed close relationships with such individuals and when I begin to share my dreams and aspirations with them, their behaviour starts to change. Some distance themselves, while others bluntly express their belief that my life goals are set too high. At times, this can be quite demotivating. However, I always manage to bounce back and redirect my focus towards my own journey of self-improvement.

The more I immerse myself in the world of influential personalities, the more I learn about people. Some things seem illogical to me, while others serve as valuable lessons and warnings. At times, I find myself feeling quite lonely, especially when I yearn to pursue greatness and surround myself with individuals who can inspire, challenge, motivate and support me in reaching my highest potential. It can be disheartening when only a few people truly believe in you and are willing to guide you towards a breakthrough. Amidst this journey, I have begun to discern the reliable sources I can wholeheartedly trust. I seek individuals who will never disappoint me and who understand that I am a woman with untapped potential, determined to ascend the ladder of success.

While many young ladies approached me to mentor them, there were a few whom I went beyond to assist them, help them change their lives for good reasons and become impactful. These are the people I will connect to my network, help those secure jobs, or pursue their dreams.

There have been periods when I wholeheartedly supported and believed in certain individuals, only to be deeply disappointed and betrayed. Some of them even went to the extent of spreading false rumours and aligning themselves with people who didn't want to see me succeed, deliberately sabotaging my progress.

Ironically, I often came across whispers and hints about their questionable behaviour before concrete evidence was presented to me. While it genuinely surprised me, I have come to realise that such incidents are not uncommon or peculiar in this world. With the passage of time, people's true character tends to reveal itself, shedding light on their intentions and actions.

The revelation of a person's character can be a profound and transformative experience, both for the individual themselves and for those around them. It is in the moments of challenge, adversity, or significant life events that true character often shines through, illuminating the essence of a person's being.

Sometimes it can be challenging to comprehend, but everyone we encounter in life is there for either a reason or a season.

We may form impressions of others based on superficial attributes, such as their appearance, social status, or achievements. However, moments of truth that these surface-level perceptions can be shattered or affirmed, revealing the true nature of an individual in due course.

Due to people's labelling and stigmatisation beliefs, the unveiling of someone's character occurs gradually, over time, as we observe their consistent actions, values and the way they treat others. It is through their words and deeds that their true colours begin to emerge. We can witness acts of kindness, compassion, integrity and honesty, which form the foundation of their character. These individuals demonstrate unwavering principles and a deep sense of moral and ethical responsibility.

However, there are moments when the character is suddenly thrust into the spotlight, driven by circumstances that demand a response. It is during these critical junctures that we witness the depth of someone's character, as they confront adversity, overcome challenges or make difficult choices. When faced with adversity, courage, resilience and determination can reveal people's true colours.

With my resilient character, I consistently transcend challenging situations, exhibiting grace under pressure and an unwavering dedication to my values. However, identifying individuals who exhibit cruelty, wickedness, or selfishness, traits that reflect their negative character, can be a daunting task. It becomes even more complex when attempting to differentiate between those who authentically reveal their true nature upon initial encounters and those who are merely putting on a facade, eventually unveiling their genuine character.

Moreover, the character can also be illuminated through acts of selflessness and sacrifice. When individuals put the needs of others before their own, their true character comes to light. They exhibit empathy, generosity, and a genuine concern for the well-being of those around them. I believe that acts of kindness reflect a deep-seated goodness that resonates with others and inspires them to follow suit.

All the same, I strongly believe that people have the capacity to change and grow. Therefore, I tend to give people the benefit of the doubt.

People have the capacity to evolve and develop their character over time. I believe a person may surprise us by displaying qualities we never anticipated, revealing hidden depths and potentials they possess. The growth can be the result of self-reflection, introspection, or life-altering experiences that challenge and shape their perspective.

The unveiling of someone's character can be a transformative and enlightening experience for both individuals and oneself. It serves as a poignant reminder of the significance of looking beyond superficial appearances, fostering empathy and acknowledging the inherent value in every person.

When an individual's true character is revealed, it possesses the potential to profoundly comprehend and inspire, motivating positive change within the world. Consequently, it is my personal conviction to allow those seeking my mentorship to come closer, gradually exposing their unique habits and distinctive traits over time.

The long-term pain I am enduring will undoubtedly serve a greater purpose.

I am a strong believer that in certain medical conditions or after undergoing surgical procedures, enduring pain may be necessary for the body's healing process.

It's understandable that it will take many years for me to fully recover or be healed or cured from all the conditions I have.

However, God could intervene to cure me instantly. By enduring pain, the person suffering may facilitate their physical recovery, allowing damaged tissues or organs to heal and regain functionality.

I also believe that enduring pain can lead to personal growth and emotional resilience. It can test one's inner strength, resilience, and ability to persevere. By enduring and navigating through challenging experiences, you will develop a deeper understanding of yourself, your capabilities and your ability to overcome adversity.

Achieving Goals and Aspirations: In some cases, individuals may choose to endure pain in pursuit of specific goals or aspirations. This could include professional ambitions, athletic endeavours, artistic achievements, or personal milestones. The pain endured may be seen as a necessary sacrifice or stepping stone towards reaching their desired outcome. As an individual who has experienced pain, I have endured so much, and I am grateful for the opportunity. I empathised with others going through similar situations. By enduring pain, they can gain a better understanding of the challenges and struggles faced by others and develop a deeper sense of compassion and empathy.

Favoured

I have endured long periods of pain based on my sense of purpose. My Christian beliefs, personal values and my sense of duty towards raising awareness on reproductive health have made me discover my purpose through the journey.

By enduring these pains, they have served as catalysts for personal growth and transformation. This has pushed me out of my comfort zone, challenged my perspectives and led me to profound changes in my life. The endurance of the pain has helped me to gain valuable insights, learn important life lessons and emerge stronger and wiser.

Truly enduring pain can serve various purposes but it is crucial to prioritise one's well-being and seek appropriate medical advice and support when dealing with prolonged or severe pain.

I am confident that the only person who I believe will never hurt me is God. As a Christian, I attribute every miracle and experience of goodness in my life to the workings of God.

On many occasions and in various circumstances, I have found myself crying out to God, desperately seeking His intervention.

During my childhood and adolescent years, I attended church every Sunday, but I must admit that I was not particularly spiritual. I did not grasp the true significance of having a personal relationship with God.

Back then, I viewed Christianity as a mere obligation, a set of rituals that one must choose to follow or just one among many religious groups available for exploration. It did not occur to me that prayer could be a source of comfort and guidance during times of distress or when faced with issues that I couldn't openly discuss with others.

However, as I have matured and encountered various challenges in life, my faith in God has increased.

My belief in God became intensive and I started worshipping God willingly. I sometimes use gospel music as my source of motivation and to overcome insecurities.

Prayers are such powerful tools that have helped me in many times of trouble.

Without prayers, I would not properly have not fully manifested my blessings.

Prayers have given me hope, made me understand my calling and have given me reassurance.

Throughout the various afflictions and painful moments of my life, I have been able to witness the boundless grace and favour of God. One significant memory that comes to mind is when my daughter was born prematurely and had to be placed in an incubator. During those weeks filled with stress and uncertainty, I clung to God's word for unwavering support.

Furthermore, I have undergone multiple surgeries, some of which seemed to offer little hope. There were instances when I believed I might not survive or wake up again. However, against all odds, I managed to pull through each of them. There was also a time when I had to face the heart-breaking experience of carrying a lifeless foetus. The path to letting go of that unborn child was far from smooth, but it was my unwavering hope in God that sustained me during that challenging period.

I may not be the typical Christian who attends church every Sunday or on a regular basis, but I make it a priority to maintain a personal and constant connection with God through prayer.

The significance of belief in God has been a topic of contemplation for individuals and societies throughout history. Although the notion of God may differ across various religious and spiritual traditions, the fundamental importance of embracing a higher power remains a consistent theme. Here are some key points that underscore the significance of believing in God:

Believing in God has given me a meaning and purpose in life. Believing in God is the concept that can help you find meaning and discover your purpose.

This belief has offered me a sense of direction and guidance in discovering my purpose on this earth. Throughout the trials and tribulations of my life, my belief in God has provided me with answers and a profound sense of fulfilment, particularly when medical practitioners refuse to listen to my plea or offer explanations.

Engaging in conversations with God has strengthened my faith, as I have found that the more I communicate with God, the stronger my belief becomes. Additionally, my faith has instilled in me a greater sense of purpose and aspirations in life.

As a human being, I firmly believe in the importance of embracing morals, respecting boundaries and staying culturally oriented, as long as these values do not infringe upon our fundamental human rights. My faith in God has deepened these principles and I am profoundly grateful for the understanding of my boundaries and the continual pursuit of personal growth each day. Through my belief, I have embraced compassion, kindness, honesty and justice, fostering harmonious relationships and nurturing a sense of social responsibility.

Moreover, my unwavering belief in God has consistently provided solace and support, acting as a source of comfort and resilience during times of hardship, grief, or uncertainty. When faced with suffering or tragedies, I turn to prayer, seeking divine breakthroughs and inner strength.

Occasionally, as I lay on my pillow, I find myself yearning for the avoidance of such tragedies in my own life, longing for relief.

I asked God for comfort, and truly, after a day or two, my faith was rebuilt and I began to see the brighter side of life. This experience has provided me with a profound sense of hope, resilience, and inner peace. It empowers individuals to navigate life's challenges and discover strength in the midst of difficult circumstances.

Religion often serves as a unifying force, bringing people together and fostering a sense of belonging within a community. Many individuals choose to attend places of worship or religious gatherings to engage in fellowship and connect with others who share similar beliefs and values. This collective experience contributes to a sense of togetherness and mutual support.

I believe places of worship give opportunities for individuals to connect with like-minded individuals who share similar values, beliefs and experiences. These communities offer support, encouragement and a sense of belonging, nurturing social connections and fostering personal growth.

Believing in God can open doors to experiences of transcendence and spiritual growth. It allows individuals to explore the realm beyond the physical and mundane, tapping into a sense of awe, wonder and the divine. Through prayer, meditation, rituals and contemplation, believers can deepen their connection with the spiritual dimension, cultivating a sense of transcendence that enhances their overall well-being.

Over the years, I have built hope and resilience during challenging times. My faith has increased and it has helped empower find courage and how to deal with difficult situations.

Being resilient has motivated me to find a powerful motivating force overcoming obstacles and maintaining a positive outlook on life.

Significantly, people find meaning and purpose in different ways and their spiritual beliefs may take various forms. The importance of belief lies in its ability to provide individuals with a sense of purpose, moral guidance, comfort, community and transcendence, ultimately enriching their lives and shaping their worldview.

And I happen to believe in God, use medication, gospel music and prayer to overcome some obstacles I may not overcome them without these tools.

Chapter 10
Shut Out Life Tragedies

As I lay on the bed, gazing at the ceiling and contemplating the intense pains coursing through my body, I struggled to comprehend the reason behind such excruciating discomfort. A searing heat engulfed my waist and lower back, accompanied by shooting pains that slowly travelled up my spine, wrapping around my hips and settling in my ovaries.

Attempting to make sense of my agony, I turned to the vast resources of the internet and researched bowel endometriosis and its associated symptoms. To my dismay, the symptoms aligned perfectly with the torment I was experiencing. However, this revelation offered little solace, as it indicated that my endometriosis was worsening despite my hopes for improvement. The additional burden of gastrointestinal distress and chronic fatigue only added to my apprehension. Nevertheless, I hold on to the glimmer of hope that I can maintain a full-time job or endure longer hours at work.

When acquaintances inquire about my professional life, I am left with no choice but to respond with a simple yet deceptive answer, assuring them that everything is going well.

Chronic pain makes it extremely difficult for me to maintain a stable job, especially considering my dream of being engaged solely in advocacy work. I constantly search the internet and job sites, but I often find that the most convenient and suitable positions are not located near me, or they are in different countries.

Although I am proud and grateful for letting go of my legal career due to the uncertainty I faced, there are moments when I experience pain or am unable to work and I start to wonder what would have happened if I had pursued becoming a lawyer. However, deep down in my heart, I know that I would not have been as passionate about my calling as a women's reproductive health advocate.

There is nothing quite like the joy that comes from knowing that others can learn from my journey and receive early medical intervention to prevent future complications. It is truly fulfilling to make a positive impact in this field.

Working in a field that ignites my passion would have been a remarkable experience and would have been a dream come true, where joy permeates every aspect of my professional life. It would have been a privilege to wake up each day with enthusiasm, knowing that I have the opportunity to engage in work that truly fulfils me and gives me joy. The joy that will accompany pursuing my passion would be unparalleled and it enriches both my personal and professional journey.

One of the greatest joys of working in a field I am passionate about is the deep sense of purpose it provides. When I am aligned with my passion, my work becomes more than just a means to earn a living. It becomes a way to make a meaningful impact and contribute to something larger than myself. Whatever career or field I chose to work in, my satisfaction from knowing that my efforts have potentially and positively influenced others and made a difference in the world would have been a privilege.

Indeed passion also fuels intrinsic motivation. It would have manifested in what I do and I genuinely love what I do, the drive to excel and improve comes naturally. Working in a field that I am passionate about would have willingly invested time and effort into improving my skills, expanding my knowledge and staying up-to-date with the latest developments in my field. Challenges and setbacks become opportunities for growth, as my passion propels me to persevere, learn from my mistakes and come back stronger. The joy of constant growth and progress adds a vibrant and fulfilling dimension to my work.

In addition, working in a field I am passionate about is the sheer enjoyment that arises from immersing myself in my work. Surely, time seems to fly and this will have made me more knowledgeable if I was to work in my field of passion for many years. I would have experienced a state of flow, where my skills and abilities are perfectly matched with the challenges at hand. This state of flow not only enhances my productivity but also brings immense joy and satisfaction, creating a harmonious and deeply fulfilling work experience.

Moreover, working in a field that I am passionate about allows me to surround myself with like-minded individuals who share my enthusiasm and drive. I would have become part of a community of individuals who inspire and support one another, fostering a sense of belonging and camaraderie. Collaborating with passionate colleagues cultivates a positive and energising work environment, where ideas flourish, creativity thrives and collective achievements are celebrated. The joy of working alongside passionate individuals is contagious and uplifts everyone involved.

Beyond the intrinsic rewards, pursuing my passion could have also led to external recognition and success. When I genuinely love what I do, I naturally invest more effort and commitment, leading to greater expertise and accomplishments. As a result, I become more likely to excel in my field, earn the respect of peers, and open doors to exciting opportunities. The satisfaction derived from external validation and the tangible fruits of my labour adds another layer of joy to my professional journey.

It is an extraordinary feeling and experience, to work in a field I am passionate about.

It infuses my work with purpose, motivates me to excel, engrosses me in a state of flow, connects me with like-minded individuals and can lead to both personal fulfilment and external success. I believe if I had found a job that gives me a totally immense passion, it would have been a testament to the profound impact that can affect my heart positive way.

I often find myself daydreaming about working a job that brings immense satisfaction and joy. While I have encountered both joyful and challenging experiences in the jobs I have undertaken, each one has provided me with valuable experiences, skills, knowledge, a wider network and new friendships.

My journey of moving to new locations and finding new jobs as an army dependent has made me more resilient. While there are advantages to being an army dependent, there are also unique challenges that come with it.

It was a week before my trip to Ghana, specifically in October 2022 and we had to relocate to Chilwell due to my husband's posting order. After completing all the packing, we were ready to explore our new house and the surrounding area. As I contemplated the situation, I reminded myself not to get too comfortable, as we might have to move once more to another location in the near future.

As an army spouse, moving around can be daunting sometimes and full of adventures.

However, there are several disadvantages and challenges that come with moving around frequently. Moving frequently has disrupted my career progression and it has made it difficult to establish myself professionally. I have often found it quite challenging to find meaningful and stable employment in a new location, although, I have excellent skills or qualifications. Sometimes they are not easily transferable.

I have noticed gaps in my employment history, which has made it challenging for new employers to understand my work experience. As a result, I have been unable to secure a stable, long-term career while my husband continues to serve in the army.

One of the main reasons for my financial strain is the frequent moving associated with my husband's military service. Each time we relocate, there are significant costs involved. I often find myself redecorating and purchasing new items to fit our new homes, which adds to the financial burden.

Additionally, settling into a new community can be financially challenging. There is a need to explore and familiarise myself with local shops, understand any restrictions and engage in recreational activities. While some of these activities may be affordable, there are instances where certain locations charge high prices for such amenities.

Frequently moving has made it challenging to establish strong social connections and form a sense of community. When I decide to establish relationships and friendships, I will have to move out and start over again in a new location.

This constant upheaval can lead to feelings of isolation, loneliness and a lack of support networks.

The employment gaps and the financial strains of moving frequently have hindered my ability to establish a stable career. It is my dream to find a position that allows me to utilise my skills and contribute to a company's success, while also accommodating the unique circumstances of my husband's military service.

In recent years, several companies have significantly expanded remote and flexible working options, leading to improved career opportunities for many army wives.

It was a chilly and damp day. As I woke up in an unfamiliar location, I glanced out of the bedroom window and noticed a row of similar houses, all detached with neatly manicured gardens. Reality sank in and I realised that I had moved from Andover and now resided in the barracks.

I gazed at the house for a few moments, silently acknowledging that this would be our new home and that I needed to adjust to the change. Just then, my daughter called out to me, reminding me that she was on a school break. Looking around the room cluttered with various moving boxes, I recalled the task at hand.

After hastily having breakfast, we delved into the task of unpacking the boxes.

As we unpacked our belongings, memories flooded back of the numerous places we have called home and the diverse experiences I have encountered. The year 2015 marked a significant milestone as we took a bold leap, relocating to Germany. Leaving my family and friends behind in the UK, I embarked on a new chapter, unsure of what lay ahead in this foreign land. However, my hopes were set on finding a better life in a different country.

Settling into the German lifestyle and adapting to the unfamiliar environment posed considerable challenges. Yet, I must acknowledge that my time in Germany has been immensely enriching and rewarding. It was during my stay there that the British Army played a crucial role in identifying my rare congenital abnormality. I am sincerely grateful for the opportunities this discovery has presented.

Had I not made the decision to move to Germany, I would not have received the necessary medical intervention and subsequent diagnosis. Without proper medical care, my symptoms could have worsened, leading to dire consequences, particularly concerning bowel endometriosis.

Although military life can be daunting at times due to constant relocation, it has also brought about significant accomplishments and provided answers to my chronic pains and illnesses. Furthermore, my work with the British Army Welfare unit has opened my eyes to the importance of welfare and meeting social needs for a fulfilling lifestyle.

Additionally, my move to Andover with the army was a joyful life experience. It provided me with the opportunity to meet Rachel, who has become like a sister to me, along with her wonderful family—her mother, Alison and her supportive husband, Jamie. They have consistently shown their support for my NGO, Speciallady Awareness. Rachel has been an incredible source of encouragement throughout.

Unfortunately, I had to relocate to Chilwell due to the military requirements when my husband was posted there. However, Rachael and I maintain regular communication despite the distance.

The British Army faces its own set of challenges, but overall, there are numerous significant benefits for individuals who are military.

Settling in Chilwell has been incredibly challenging and unsettling for me. Every day, I struggle to find activities that interest me and there are times when I simply lack the motivation to step outside and prefer staying indoors. Adding to my difficulties, my chronic pains have resurfaced, leaving me feeling extremely unwell.

The constant pain I experience has led to a significant increase in my insomnia, making it even harder to find rest and relaxation. As I dwell on the idea of living in Chilwell, I find myself becoming increasingly disinterested, yearning to return to Andover or its surrounding areas.

The only aspect that brings a glimmer of excitement is the fact that my sister resides just an hour away from Chilwell. I try to reassure myself that I will have the opportunity to visit her frequently. However, it doesn't change the fact that I genuinely miss Andover.

Andover is a town that boasts a wide range of facilities and abundant job opportunities. Additionally, it benefits from excellent transportation connections and a strong sense of community. Personally, I am captivated by the picturesque lakes and the charming surrounding towns, making it easy to commute to Wiltshire and other towns in Hampshire.

One fond memory I have is of visiting Chalton Park during moments of boredom or when I needed time for reflection and relaxation. Observing the graceful ducks swimming in the serene waters, surrounded by lush green trees and vibrant plant life, always brings me a sense of tranquillity. It's a place where I often indulge in photography, capturing the park's essence in every shot.

On occasion, I enjoy taking leisurely walks to Abbotts Ann, a delightful village located approximately two miles southwest of Andover. It's a place where I can witness the charm of the neighbouring villages, observing people elegantly riding horses or engaging in farming activities. These sights further enhance my appreciation for the countryside surrounding Andover.

Amport, the village where my daughter used to attend her primary school, 'Amport school' is a village green which is surrounded by thatched cottages. We used to enjoy country walks, there were many attractive routes.

I decided to conduct further research on Chilwell, Beeston and the surrounding areas in order to explore the attractions and activities available, similar to those found in Hampshire. I discovered that there are several noteworthy historical sites and beautiful lakes in the area. During our stay, we can plan to visit some of these lakes and explore the historical places.

Whenever I express my dissatisfaction to my sister, she reminds me that I haven't been living in this area for very long and assures me that I will gradually adjust and become more accustomed to it as time goes on.

After some reflection, I came to the realisation that as a military wife, it is not always guaranteed that we will be posted to areas that I personally enjoy. However, I understand that it's essential for me to give my best effort and adapt to the new surroundings, even though it may take some time to adjust. It is crucial to acknowledge the effects of frequent moves and embrace the military lifestyle.

Notably, I found myself increasingly worried about my health due to persistent lower back and waist pain. Despite attempting various stretches and exercises, I was unable to achieve the relaxation or pain-free lifestyle I desired. This caused my anxiety to escalate on a daily basis as I desperately searched for solutions.

To make matters worse, my sleeping habits were also disrupted, leaving me feeling utterly hopeless about the entire situation. I yearned to understand the cause of this sudden relapse and how it would impact my work routine.

In an attempt to find a suitable solution, I began researching part-time and flexible job opportunities. However, most of the available options either required full-time hours or failed to meet the necessary requirements for accommodating my health needs.

Every time I searched online for jobs, I fervently hoped to stumble upon suitable opportunities. While I have had some promising interviews, the majority of them have been geared towards hiring permanent full-time employees. This realisation has reminded me once again that part-time positions are not easy to come by. Additionally, I have been seeking jobs that would allow me to take breaks and stretch without straining my back.

Navigating through this challenging situation triggered memories of a time when I possessed greater strength and could undertake any job without limitations. I reminisce about my days attending university, working diligently and still managing to enjoy outings with friends. I was incredibly active and rarely experienced fatigue. In hindsight, I wish I had exerted more effort and saved enough money to secure a better future.

The process of maturing is unpredictable, as it brings about various life events that prompt us to ponder and sometimes regret our past decisions and youthful indiscretions. If only I had been aware of the long-term repercussions of my childhood illnesses.

I would have taken precautions and carefully planned my future. I would have made my health a top priority in every decision I made, whether it be related to my career, relationships, marriage, or daily lifestyle.

Your Circle Determines Your Future

Throughout my journey as a reproductive health advocate and mentor to youth, I have learnt that in order to be an exemplary figure to others, it is essential to exhibit certain characteristics and traits that inspire trust, foster confidence and facilitate reliability.

Being a relatable voice requires more than just sharing one's personal journey. It also depends on how others perceive you and the image you project to the public. Therefore, it is crucial to cultivate qualities that resonate with people on multiple levels.

One important aspect of this process has been my ability to filter out distractions and distance myself from individuals who do not contribute to my personal growth. By doing so, I have created a space where I can thrive and focus on my mission.

Furthermore, I have come to understand the significance of surrounding myself with like-minded individuals who share similar visions and goals. These are the people who recognise that how we choose to spend our time on a daily basis directly impacts our future.

By embodying these principles and aligning myself with individuals who share my values, I have been able to establish myself as a trusted voice in the field of reproductive health advocacy.

I have participated in activities and pursued work that nourishes my mind in a positive way, providing me with excellent networking opportunities. However, achieving these results did not happen overnight; it required consistent effort, perseverance and unwavering commitment.

Over time, I have encountered instances where people commented on the changes they perceived in me. Some of them have noticed that I no longer attend their events such as weddings, birthday celebrations or gatherings. The truth is I had to consciously work on my mindset and become selective about the people I engage with, the places I go and the purpose behind every task I undertake.

While it is undoubtedly valuable to have friends and associates around, it is crucial to consider how they influence your thinking, life choices, goals and visions. As renowned influential personalities often assert, your circle of connections has a significant impact on defining who you are and shaping your destiny. While some may argue that these statements are not entirely accurate, they hold a considerable amount of truth.

There were times in my life when I did not carefully consider my life choices or actions. As a result, I often found myself distressed, losing money or losing good friends. However, when I reflect on the past, I am incredibly grateful for how far I have come and how my mindset has evolved.

I am grateful that I made the decision to change my circle of friends and focus more on my purpose. By practising this, I have encountered amazing individuals from whom I have learnt valuable lessons. It's as if we are magnets attracting like-minded people and it's our choice to decide who we allow into our lives. If we believe we cannot change our ways of life, we become complacent with our current lifestyle.

There is nothing wrong with staying true to who you are. However, I made a conscious decision to change my life because I realised the old way of living was not aligned with the future I envisioned for myself.

Moreover, going through the uncertainty journey, enduring countless hospital admissions, multiple surgeries and facing various complications have profoundly changed my mind set for the better.

While I understand that the people we surround ourselves with can influence our lives and shape our experiences, I would not say that our circle defines who we are entirely. As individuals, we have unique personalities, beliefs, values and life experiences that contribute to our identity. While our relationships and interactions with others certainly play a role in our personal growth and development, they do not solely determine who we are.

Our identities are influenced by a variety of factors such as our upbringing, education, cultural background, personal choices and individual traits. Sometimes it is not easy to change your identity due to how you were brought up or what you have been programmed to be. It may be possible to change but it will require a substantial amount of hard work and commitment.

Truly your circle of friends, family and acquaintances can have an impact on you, this is why a person should see the importance of recognising that how they live their lives or feed their mind may have the ability to shape their own lives and define who they are.

Moreover, the types of relationships we encourage around us have a huge influence on our decisions and choices.

Ultimately, who we are is a combination of various elements, including our relationships but also extending beyond them. We are constantly evolving and growing as individuals who are influenced by both internal and external factors.

We have the choice to determine our own values, goals and paths in life.

Nevertheless, as I faced challenging situations, I learnt who my true friends were. I have come to value good working relationships more and now have a smaller circle of close friends. Throughout my life, various individuals have entered and influenced it, both positively and negatively.

One thing I am grateful for is my ability to recognise negative or toxic people and relationships. However, due to my kind-hearted nature, I sometimes find myself entertaining certain individuals out of pity. There was a period in my life when I had such a friend who seemed to thrive on toxic relationships and she surrounded herself with negative people. It seemed that every time we met, she had issues with someone. Even her intimate relationships were toxic. I was the kind of friend who genuinely wanted to see her succeed. I yearned for her to become an exemplary woman and a remarkable leader.

She undeniably possesses remarkable skills; however, it is unfortunate that she allowed negativity to overshadow her talents. Regrettably, she would often invest her time in pursuits that did not serve a meaningful purpose.

It took me a considerable amount of time to realise that this individual was spreading false rumours about me. There comes a point in life when it becomes clear that toxic surroundings are no longer needed.

It is disheartening when you genuinely care about someone, only to discover that they harbour ill intentions towards you. All I ever wanted was to positively impact a friend's life through good deeds. I am grateful to God for blessing me with such a gift.

Anyone who gets closer to me can attest that my intentions are always for the best interests of others. Regrettably, this sincerity has led to negative outcomes in the past.

The year 2023 was becoming increasingly exciting and I truly believed in it. I found myself eagerly counting down the months, hoping time would pass more quickly. The feeling of anticipation was strong within me.

I am deeply impressed and proud of the hard work and determination that allowed me to overcome obstacles and shape my own narrative. Reflecting back on my childhood, I could not help but recall the immense pain and countless trials I endured.

As my birthday approached, I began to envision how I would celebrate it, hoping to make it truly remarkable and unforgettable. Additionally, I felt a strong desire to contribute to Speciallady Awareness work and engage in meaningful initiatives. I had planned to celebrate my birthday by dedicating a few weeks to these endeavours.

Fortieth Birthday: Celebrating my 40th birthday is a significant milestone that holds great importance to me, although I felt happy about being 40 years old, I am afraid of growing old without leaving a legacy.

Irrespective of what you do, developing a community or company is what is paramount.

As I thought that turning 40 was a great opportunity, I believe that this has given me the opportunity to reflect on my life journey so far. It is a time to celebrate personal achievements, both personally and professionally.

I have accomplished some great things and I have always been thankful for the opportunities. I believe that at 40 years.

I know the good God has been good to me.

I have been able to accomplish great experiences and I am grateful for achieving personal growth, nurturing relationships and some career advancements.

Definitely, turning 40 years old has made me acknowledge these accomplishments. Therefore, I gladly celebrate this milestone since I have gained wisdom and a considerable amount of life experience.

I have noticed I am keen on sharing my life experiences with others, advising, mentoring and guiding the younger generation.

As I recognised how far I have come, it gave me an opportunity to reflect on the learnt lessons and pass on valuable knowledge to younger people and loved ones.

Surely, I am grateful for every family member, my friends, whoever I have worked with and my mentees.

As I mark my 40th birthday, I would like to express appreciation and gratitude to my friends, family members, colleagues past and present and anyone who has supported and contributed to my personal growth and success over the years.

As I grow, I have learnt to prioritise my personal well-being and indulge in activities that bring joy and fulfilment.

My main important thing to do as a leader is self-care. Knowing when to rest and what to do is very crucial especially when you have goals and visions. I have developed a habit of walking near the lakes, going to a spa, travelling to different countries, sightseeing, etc.

I have realised that turning 40 years old has served as a reminder to prioritise self-care, embrace change and approach the future with a positive mindset.

These activities have had a positive impact on me.

This milestone has reminded me of the importance of emotional, physical and mental health. Also, it is a transitional phase in my life, which has allowed me to embrace change and embark on new beginnings.

My coming 40th birthday has taught me to accept the passage of time and to approach the future with optimism and enthusiasm.

I have achieved an opportunity to set new goals, make positive lifestyle changes and embrace the opportunities that lie ahead of me.

My 40th birthday was a wake-up call, prompting me to reflect on my past activities and behaviour. It made me realise the importance of understanding my calling and purpose on this earth. This milestone has solidified my belief in me and my potential.

I made a conscious effort to come up with ideas to mark my 40th.

Chapter 11
New Life

I decided to celebrate my 40th birthday by organising a charity football tournament aimed at raising awareness about the importance of early medical intervention and supporting youth empowerment. I wanted to mark this milestone in a way that would make a meaningful impact on society.

I was particularly concerned about the lack of access to healthcare and sanitary products for many women, especially during their menstruation. Therefore, through this football tournament, we hoped to raise funds and increase awareness in this area.

When I discussed this idea with my friend Alex, who is already involved with NGOs specialising in this field, he was thrilled to join me in organising the charity football tournament. Another friend, Yussif Chibsah, also expressed his interest and together, we decided to embark on this charitable endeavour.

We reached out to several renowned Ghanaian footballers based in the UK as well as some in Ghana and they have shown great enthusiasm to participate in the tournament.

The preparation was quite demanding, but we knew that with hard work and dedication, we would overcome every obstacle we encountered and deliver an excellent outcome to the public. All of my previous tasks and endeavours have always turned out successfully, although organising them was not easy. However, I never gave up or got distracted until I achieved a great outcome.

We divided the various tasks among ourselves in organising the tournament, ensuring that each one of us had specific tasks to complete within a reasonable time frame.

We agreed to invite dignitaries from the UK, Ghana, renowned Ghanaian footballers, the Commonwealth Youth Council etc.

We discussed how we can collaborate with international organisations like UNICEF, Commonwealth Youth Council, Chiefs, Queens, the current ruling political party in Ghana and the Political Party in opposition including members of the public. We plan to host four thousand guests at the Queen Elizabeth Stadium in Enfield. We intended to seek partnerships with Enfield Town Football Club and other organisations.

I started conducting online research, exploring various event pages to gather information about football tournaments and gain some insights. Meanwhile, my partners and I were actively involved in organising the tournament and sharing our innovative ideas. I made sure to jot down all the valuable tips, comments, and suggestions pertaining to the tasks that awaited us. Although the magnitude of the event was daunting, I maintained a positive outlook and firmly believed in its potential for success.

In April 2023, an organisation called the National Academy of Students Achievement Awards in Ghana, with whom I have previously collaborated on community projects, extended an invitation to my NGO to participate in their career and capacity development summit. The event took place at the Ghana Institute of Journalism, Ghana Communication Technology University, Winneba University, and Valley View University.

One of our dedicated volunteers, Anna, was selected to speak at these universities, highlighting the importance of early medical intervention and sharing information about the initiatives of Speciallady Awareness. The university tours were a resounding success and I was delighted to receive positive feedback from the rest of the team regarding Anna's exceptional confidence and excellent presentation skills.

This made me realise that I had successfully trained my team to continue working while I was in the UK. Another notable instance was in May during Menstrual Hygiene Awareness Day when I assigned Sylvia Davis to oversee our annual menstrual hygiene and health outreach. We selected a school in the eastern region of Ghana, Apeguso Senior and Junior Secondary School, which had a student population of over a thousand girls. Our objective was to distribute sanitary products to thousands of female students while educating them about menstrual hygiene.

Sylvia excelled in her role as the project coordinator. She demonstrated exceptional skills in sourcing affordable sanitary products from wholesalers, coordinating logistics and accompanying the team to the eastern region to spearhead the outreach project. Additionally, she delivered impactful presentations to the students, leaving a lasting impression. I was truly astounded by the positive feedback I received regarding her remarkable professionalism. It was truly a blessing to have such dedicated and hardworking individuals on the Speciallady Awareness team.

When I have access to all this good news, my gratitude grows even stronger, knowing that I no longer have to worry about frequent travel to Ghana for outreach projects. Funding has been challenging and the money that would have been spent on tickets, transportation and logistics can now be used to purchase more items for donation. By training more volunteers, they can become knowledgeable and confident in public speaking, effectively delivering crucial information about the importance of seeking early medical intervention and highlighting the potential consequences of late diagnosis and unnecessary surgeries.

It is my ultimate aspiration to see Speciallady Awareness become a reputable and dynamic charitable organisation that is globally recognised for its impactful initiatives. I firmly believe that one day, my dreams will materialise and I will reflect upon my journey with a deep sense of purpose and fulfilment. I am aware that some people may be taken aback when I express my vision of Speciallady Awareness achieving global recognition. It is possible that they perceive it as mere daydreaming and advise me to abandon such lofty aspirations. However, I have unwavering faith that the same God that has guided and protected me thus far will continue to bestow blessings upon me, including the realisation of these aspirations.

I believe being born with uterus didelphys was a blessing in disguise and it has given my life purpose and meaning. Every situation we encounter is not a matter of mere chance; rather, God knew each one of us even before we were formed in our mother's womb.

While I acknowledge that some of my wishes may seem unrealistic at times, deep within me, I hold firm faith that my desires will be fulfilled. I understand that it requires unwavering belief, diligent effort, unwavering focus and a commitment to never give up.

When I started Speciallady Awareness, I had to sell my shoes and clothes to raise the initial funding necessary to purchase sanitary products. However, today I no longer need to resort to such measures, regardless of the challenges the NGO has faced. Instead, I have chosen to write proposals to numerous organisations, businesses and potential donors to seek their support. Throughout this journey of becoming an advocate, I have acquired a wealth of knowledge and wisdom in the field of humanitarian work.

Many people often ask me how I manage to maintain consistency in my work and stay focused. I am amazed when I see the continuous progress of Speciallady Awareness and how far we have come. It seems that our work keeps expanding with each passing period and we never cease to astonish people with our persistent efforts.

I must admit that I do not often share with people the challenges I face, such as staying awake during sleepless nights when insomnia strikes. Instead of succumbing to restlessness, I choose to utilise those moments to research topics related to reproductive health education, learn how to write proposals and articles and enhance my skills.

There are days when I find myself writing countless emails, only to receive rejections in return. However, I remain undeterred and continue to persevere. Rejections are a natural part of the journey and I believe that each rejection brings me closer to an acceptance.

I write to bigger organisations in similar fields to collaborate with them, yet some would not reply and others want me to join them in fundraising. I have previously joined some to fundraise which was rewarding however; I would like them to also consider my request.

But whenever I get rejections, it rather pushes me to work harder on myself and my NGO Speciallady Awareness.

I believe that facing challenges is crucial for me to appreciate the blessings and achievements I have attained so far. Practising this belief consistently motivates me to never give up and continuously explore excellent opportunities in my advocacy work.

We live in a world where very few people truly believe in your dreams and push you to grow mentally, emotionally or financially. People tend to relate to you more when you experience a breakthrough in life. Hence, I have made the decision to focus on improving myself on a daily basis. This way, when I meet people who genuinely want to support or contribute to my growth, I am prepared.

Furthermore, it is quite normal for individuals to desire association with those who contribute to their growth, as building a legacy and a good reputation requires considerable effort. I used to perceive prominent individuals as being stuck up until I began taking small steps towards reaching my own goals. This journey has required financial investment, time, sacrifices, a shift in mindset and a change in my social circle, acquaintances and overall perspective on life. The path is often challenging and unsettling, but the rewards justify the pain, sacrifices, and sorrow. Undoubtedly, building resilience and navigating the path to greatness is not easy.

One afternoon in April, I found myself lying in bed, anxiously checking my phone every thirty minutes, hoping for a call from the hospital. I had recently undergone urine tests and I was waiting for confirmation if my health issues were indeed related to my kidneys. With each passing moment, my heart rate subtly increased, yet I tried to reassure myself that everything would be alright. The mere thought of having kidney problems was distressing and I yearned for the hospital's confirmation to provide me with a sense of certainty, even though I was already experiencing pain. As my mind dwelt on the potential kidney diseases the consultant suspected, my worries intensified.

When I finally spoke to the hospital's correspondence, I was thrilled when she mentioned that the urine test came back clear.

This made me realise that life is fleeting and in the blink of an eye, anything can happen. Therefore, I must strive for happiness, fully embrace life and diligently work towards creating a lasting legacy for my generation.

While growing up, I used to envision myself as a wealthy woman living in a million-pound house, surrounded by expensive furniture and luxuries. However, I soon discovered that achieving such a lifestyle required significant breakthroughs, consistent discipline, hard work and networking.

Regrettably, I neglected the importance of learning financial intelligence during my younger years, only realising later in life that there was so much I had yet to grasp. Financial intelligence, in particular, eluded me, despite being a crucial and practical life skill. I never anticipated reaching a point where I would yearn for essential knowledge and life skills.

Nevertheless, I consider myself incredibly fortunate to witness the abundance of blessings in my life today.

Tomorrow is unpredictable and too often we neglect the fact that nobody knows what the future holds. What truly matters is the actions we take today, as they will shape our future and define who we become.

Having said that is crucial to prioritise investing in your future and yourself.

However, it is during these unpredictable moments that we often find ourselves faced with choices. We have the choice to embrace the obstacles and perceive them as opportunities for growth or improvement.

We need to learn from every obstacle to discover new passions, ideas and talents.

If I had not experienced a long health uncertainty, I would not have become a woman reproductive health advocate or founded Speciallady Awareness or become an inspiration to other women suffering in silence with gynaecological conditions.

It is undeniable that embracing the unpredictability of life is not always easy. It can be frightening and unsettling, particularly when we face unforeseen setbacks or disappointments.

But this is what will enable a person to become resilient by building strength to overcome such uncertainties.

The key to living a fulfilling life lies in embracing your true self and nurturing a positive mindset.

Reflecting on my life, I do not see why I should complain about the setbacks and traumas I have encountered. These challenges have served as the very catalysts for my blessings, achievements and ultimate triumphs. The pain, obstacles and trauma I experienced served as powerful motivators, propelling me towards becoming the best version of myself. I firmly believe that without these challenges, I would not have attained the level of greatness I have reached today.

To earn the title of 'The Special Lady', I had to traverse these arduous paths, which taught me valuable lessons, bestowed upon me wisdom and shaped me into the woman I am today. My experiences derive from countless individuals, inspiring them to believe that regardless of their social background, medical complications or circumstances at birth, they too can make a positive impact on the world.

They were brought into this world with a purpose, a purpose that often reveals itself through the experience of difficulties. Therefore, when confronted with adversity, it is most beneficial to perceive them as opportunities for personal growth and triumph. Concentrating on the negative aspects of situations only exacerbates the challenges and does not contribute to effectively overcoming adversity.

Be inspired.